RISK&
GROW
RICH

RISK&
GROW
RICH

How to Make Millions in Real Estate

KENDRA TODD

with Charles Andrews

ReganBooks
An Imprint of HarperCollins*Publishers*

To our readers and to anyone with the courage to dare a great dream . . . may this book inspire you to overcome your fears, discover what you're capable of, and reach the goals that make your life extraordinary.

HarperCollins books may be purchased for educational, business, or sales promotional use. For information please write: Special Markets Department, HarperCollins Publishers Inc., 10 East 53rd Street, New York, NY 10022.

FIRST EDITION

Printed on acid-free paper
Library of Congress Cataloging-in-Publication Data

Todd, Kendra.
    Risk & grow rich : 10 steps to real success / Kendra Todd, with Charles Andrews.—1st ed.
        p.   cm.
    ISBN-13: 978-0-06-089972-1 (alk. paper)
    ISBN-10:   0-06-089972-7 (alk. paper)
    1. Investments.   2. Risk management.   3. Real estate investment—United States.
I. Title: Risk and grow rich.   II. Andrews, Charles B., 1971–   III. Title.
HG4521.T63   2006
332.6—dc22   2006042336

06 07 08 09 10 RRD 10 9 8 7 6 5 4 3 2 1

CONTENTS

INTRODUCTION

THE WILD, WILD WEST

By Charles Andrews

Even while we speak, envious time has passed: seize the day, putting as little trust as possible in tomorrow!

HORACE, ODE I–XI, "CARPE DIEM"

I'm on a flight back to my beloved South Florida, but I can't help thinking about the rust-red Spring Mountains topped by Mt. Charleston, drier air than I had ever imagined, endless sunrises, and nights illuminated by a billion neon lights. I'm talking, of course, about Las Vegas. Or as younger people, influenced by the film *Swingers,* love to say, "Vegas, baby!"

My first trip to Las Vegas was a revelation. Not because of the gambling or the entertainment; I had seen plenty of both in my time. But because of the incredible growth of the area and what it meant to someone who made his living as I did, by locating outstanding real estate investments for my clients and for myself. What I saw in Las Vegas was a new, wild frontier, a place that had turned itself into a colossal travel destination and was now on its way to reinventing itself as the world's new resort megacity, a Miami Beach under the blazing sun of the Nevada desert. The city's defiance of conventional wisdom about growth and its seemingly unlimited potential make it the perfect emblem of one of the most important principles in wealth building: *you must go where the market is.*

I bring up this story because in *Risk & Grow Rich,* Kendra and I are going to share with you what we have learned about leveraging risk to create wealth from our personal real estate investment experiences and from our work with our company, MyHouseRE.com. Started in 2000, My HouseRE.com is also in the business of defying conventional wisdom by helping real estate investors find shortcuts to wealth by buying condominium conversions and preconstruction condos in areas with strong fundamentals that are likely to appreciate greatly in the future. But what we really do is educate our clients. I like to say we defy the old maxim that real estate is about location, location, location. I say it's about *education, education, education.* How can you know if a location is right unless you've learned about the area, the economy, proposed future development, and population trends? You can't. Education enables you to take smart risks that look crazy to people who don't have the same information. It's information that has led Kendra and me to expand our business to where the market is, namely, the West.

Believe me, there are no bigger South Florida boosters than the two of us. It's a wonderful place to live and the real estate market here creates opportunities to build wealth everywhere you look. But what's happening in the West, especially in Las Vegas, is nothing short of unbelievable. Here are a few of the statistics:

— According to the Las Vegas Chamber of Commerce, the city is the fastest growing in the United States, with an estimated two acres of land developed every twenty-four hours and 6,000 people every month moving to the city permanently.

— According to the *Boston Globe,* since 2000, the median price of a new home in Las Vegas (excluding condo conversions) has more than doubled, from $161,893 to $335,091.

— As of late 2005, a total of ninety-three luxury condominium projects, with 194 towers and 51,000 housing units, had been proposed or were being built, says Brian Gordon of Applied Analysis, a Las Vegas research firm.

— The South Strip is booming at an unprecedented rate, with huge projects like the luxury condominium/casino project Las Ramblas, backed in part by actor George Clooney, poised to change the landscape of the city.

These ultra-swank luxury townhomes and condos are not for the hourly wage workers of the casinos. They are meant for wealthy regular visitors, retirees who want second homes—and investors like you. There is no place else in the country where you can find preconstruction or conversion real estate at price points that offer such value with such promise of appreciation. All the signs point to Las Vegas's continuing to grow and the South Strip and the well-known Strip meeting, like the two halves of the Transcontinental Railroad, in four to six years. When that happens, investors with the foresight to buy early should see exceptional profits.

The point of all this, other than to clue you into a wonderful real estate market, is to illustrate that making your first million by the time you turn forty—or before—means having the vision to recognize emerging markets early and taking the risk of moving into them before they have been proved "safe" by others. Waiting until a market is "safe" inevitably means that the price goes up and your return on investment, or ROI, goes down. You've got to educate yourself, learn the telltale signs of a boom in the making, and then act quickly with a system in mind. That's what we do at My HouseRE.com. Kendra and I understand that you can't create a market; you can only recognize it and take advantage of it before others do.

Of course, Bugsy Siegel was an exception to this rule; he created the market because it didn't exist. He wasn't the first person to look out at the desert of southern Nevada and see a tourism paradise of gaming, liquor, and sex; he was just the first one to recognize that Nevada's legalization of gambling gave it the potential to be the adult playground that the post–World War II generation would line up for. Bugsy found a partner and created The Flamingo, the first of what would become hundreds of garish, exciting resorts that would turn that barren stretch of wasteland into Sin City.

Siegel created the market, but it was a market that, to this day, makes its own rules. Most cities have to worry about where the resources are coming from before they can grow at even a moderate pace. Not Las Vegas. The attitude there is that "growth is good," and the bulldozers are leveling land and laying infrastructure before anyone's sure where the water will come from. The normal rules don't seem to apply. The architecture is wild and fanciful, the laws are . . . let's say *relaxed,* and the sheer volume of people streaming into the city to make their fortunes can leave you feeling overwhelmed. It's not much different in other sunny playgrounds of the West. Arizona, particularly the areas around Yuma and Scottsdale, continue to experience its own boom, with U.S. Census Bureau data predicting 3.1 million more people in the state by 2020. Liberal Austin, Texas, home of the late Stevie Ray Vaughan and Dell Computer, saw its population grow 48 percent between 1990 and 2000, according to the Census Bureau. Even in southern California, one of the most expensive markets in the country, there are opportunities if you know where to look. Everybody wants to be where the weather is warm and the humidity is low.

You have to be prepared to jump and go where the market is. This may not mean hitting the road for another city; we're planning to open an office in Las Vegas but not actually move there. But it can mean a physical move, or it can just mean putting forth the resources to compete in a new market—research, marketing, salespeople, networking. You can't control a market, but you can control your response to one. That's what we've done in responding to the incredible potential of Las Vegas. We could have stayed in South Florida and Orlando and been very profitable, but instead we've chosen to risk by adding the West to our portfolio, and that's going to make us and our clients very rich.

It's important to add that even though you move into a new market, you shouldn't change the way you do business. I am neither a gambler nor a cowboy. Nor is Kendra. Everything we do and teach our clients is methodical and strategic, and that hasn't changed because we're part of the new Gold Rush taking place on Las Vegas Boulevard. It's tempting. But it's vital that you stick with your fundamentals and do business your way, in a way that reduces your risk and keeps you from becoming stressed and discouraged. In Vegas, you can throw a stone in any direction and hit a guy offering you a "can't-miss" deal that represents an unhealthy risk. Some would jump at that deal; we don't. We have a formula and we stick to it. In the last chapter, we'll share that formula with you.

I've said I'm not a gambler. That's true when it comes to casinos and real estate deals. But there are things I will gamble on: ROI calculations, cash-on-cash return, land feasibility studies, appreciation in residential real estate, population demographics, and good old-fashioned gut instinct, honed by years of experience, about where to guide our investors. Kendra and I will both gamble that those data, backed by our own knowledge about the market, make the risks we take on smart, wise, and profitable. And when you're gambling in the Wild, Wild West, those are the best results you can hope for.

CHARLES ANDREWS

1.

HOW RISK BECAME A FOUR-LETTER WORD

Two roads diverged in a wood, and I . . .
I took the one less traveled by,
and that has made all the difference.

ROBERT FROST, "THE ROAD NOT TAKEN"

Have you ever heard of Lewis Morris? You should have. He was one of the signers of the Declaration of Independence. He was one in a long, proud line of risk takers in the history of what became the United States, going back to the Pilgrims of 1620 and the early settlers of the North American wilderness.

Morris was a landholder from New York who put his name at the bottom of that world-changing piece of parchment on August 2, 1776 (that's right; the Declaration was dated July 4 but not signed until a month later).

He and the other signers (there were fifty-six in all, though John Hancock tends to be the only one we recall) must have known the risk they were taking. They were affixing their names to a document that was a direct challenge to British rule over the American colonies. They were marking themselves as targets for the rage and retribution of the Crown. In some cases, they were signing their death warrants.

Why did they do it? Most were comfortable landowners, which in colonial America was the main measure of wealth. British rule had been kind to these men, yet they were willing to put their fortunes and futures on the line for the cause. I think the answer is the same as the answer we give today when someone asks us why we take a risk: because the promise of reward outweighs the potential dangers. Either that, or what we want to achieve is so precious that we have no choice but to risk everything to go for it.

That was the motivation for Morris and the other signers. They saw independence as a possibility, so they put themselves on the firing line to achieve it. And some of them did pay dearly. Nine died in battle. Many had their homes destroyed or lost their businesses. Morris saw his estate burned by British soldiers, his livestock killed, and his family forced into exile. He worked for years trying to rebuild his farm and served on the first Board of Regents for the University of New York, and died in 1798 at 72.

> **"The only lost cause is one we give up on before we enter the struggle."**
>
> **Vaclav Havel, in Amnesty International's essay "From Prisoner to President—A Tribute"**

Lewis Morris paid a high price for his risk—but, of course, the goal was realized. Whenever I think a risk is too great for me, I look at the example of people like Morris and others and think what they were risking to achieve their ends.

DO YOU SEE THE OPPORTUNITY OR THE HAZARD?

This book is about the power that taking wise, calculated, and mitigated risks has to transform lives. But before we can even begin to talk about the power of risk, we've got to take a long, hard look at the fear of risk. I'm a natural risk taker. Most people aren't. I was fortunate enough to have parents who not only encouraged me to try new things, but pushed me into unfamiliar territory, always with the mantra, "You can do it." I grew up playing soccer, basketball, field hockey, you name it. When I was in the eighth grade, my dad entered my team into a basketball tournament against teams that had great training, and we were playing against a team on which the girls were seven inches taller than we were. We played with heart and we won, even though no one thought we could. However, the vast majority of people in our culture have been taught to look on risk as something to fear, something to avoid. That's exactly the wrong approach to take if you want to have a rewarding, fulfilling life.

Fear of risk is programmed into our brains. It's a survival mechanism that makes sense if you think about evolution. When they were scattered throughout the savannas of East Africa in pre-agrarian hunter-gatherer tribes, our distant ancestors did everything in groups. The men hunted together. The women and children gathered roots and plants together. There was safety in numbers; alone, you were much more vulnerable to predators and accidents. Those who played it safe were rewarded with survival and the opportunity to pass on their genes to the next generation. We're hard-wired to avoid risk.

Fast forward to today. We no longer fight for pure survival. Most of us have jobs, families, and responsibilities, but we live in a world where technology, economics, and freedom combine to make risk taking more worthwhile—and less life-threatening—than ever. If you're a smart graduate student, there's nothing stopping you from dropping out halfway to your Ph.D., running up your credit cards to start an Internet company with your buddies, and turning it into a billion-dollar juggernaut. Ever hear of Google? That's how that company came to be. And if your company crashes and burns? You don't get eaten. You regroup, go back to school, and spend a few years paying off debt.

Unfortunately, we still look at risk from the perspective of the early hominid whose sole priority each day was to survive. Present your average working Joe with a business proposition that has some risk to it but also has a big potential payoff and his eyes are going to zoom right to the risk. The first thought in his head is going to be about all the ways things could backfire and end in disaster. He might not even see past the hazard to the potential payoff. He'll never discover that if things don't fall apart, he stands to make a ton of money and be better able to support his family. His knee-jerk reaction to the idea of risk is negative: "This is how this could hurt me." That's the reaction of 90 percent of the population.

Have you ever watched poker on TV or played it yourself? The most fascinating aspect of the game is not the cards, but what goes on the minds of the elite players, guys like Chris Ferguson and Daniel Negreanu. When they're looking at a hand and deciding to bet or fold, they're making numerous calculations in their heads. One of them is "pot odds." With pot odds, you look at the amount of money in the pot and compare that to the size of the bet you'll have to make to stay in the hand. The more you can win with a small bet, the better your pot odds. Combine this awareness with knowledge of how many cards (or "outs") can give you a winning hand and you've got the tools to minimize your risk and maximize your chance of a reward.

THINK LIKE A POKER PLAYER

To achieve the goals closest to your heart, you've got to start thinking like a poker player. You've got to look rationally at the risk, but also at the possible payoff and the possible obstacles in your way and make your decision based on that information. That's what the most successful people in the world do.

That doesn't mean it's easy. In a January 2004 survey by Pricewater-houseCoopers, nearly 1,400 CEOs said that while they were aware that smart, aggressive risk taking was critical to their companies' growth, they were worried about the barriers to that risk taking. Even huge corporations have an aversion to risk, despite the fact that the last 100 years of business have shown again and again that the businessperson who sticks his or her neck out and innovates will, by and large, be the one with the billion-dollar net worth and the private island.

Jeff Bezos is a perfect example. The founder of Amazon.com was called a visionary by some and a fool by others when he launched his online bookstore in 1995. The "experts" (we'll talk later about why you should never listen to them) said he could never sell enough books online to turn a profit. Later, when he added everything from DVDs to home and garden supplies, they said he was nuts, that he could never compete with Wal-Mart. After the dotcom crash in 2001, the experts assumed Amazon would dry up. But Bezos persisted, continuing to grow his business through the hard times when the stock was worth peanuts. The experts still predicted doom and gloom.

Today, Amazon.com has a market cap of between $40 billion and $50 billion. It's one of the biggest brands in the world, not just on the Web. The opposite of the "Wal-Mart effect" has happened; Wal-Mart has tried to compete with Amazon online, where its renowned supply chain methods don't give it any advantage, and has been trounced. Amazon has become the first place people go when they're looking for almost anything online. Jeff Bezos stuck his neck out, withstood the screams of shareholders who wanted quick profits, and prevailed. Now he's a billionaire, and I don't think anyone doubts the viability of his company anymore.

My point is that there's a formula for success in any venture in life, if you have the awareness and courage to follow it. Kendra's Risk/Reward Equation:

(Smart Risk + Reward Assessment + Research and Planning)	x	Persistent, Consistent Action	=	Positive Results

Let's break that down so it's completely clear.

— **SMART RISK** means the risk you're looking at fits your goals and reflects a modicum of sense. You might not know if the risk is worthwhile until you start digging and analyzing the data, but you know if it fits your objectives, your skill set, and your resources. For example, I invest personally in residential property; I know a lot about it and I'm good at it. So if someone came to me with a can't-miss deal involving investing in a restaurant, I'd walk away. I don't know the restaurant business, so the risks are too high. I wouldn't even waste my time on research. It's too far outside what a CEO might call my "core competency."

Questions to ask: Is this risk too far outside my comfort zone? Would I be considered a novice in the field? Does the risk get me closer to my stated goals? Do I have any resources already in place related to this area?

— **REWARD ASSESSMENT** means you have calculated whether or not the potential reward involved makes the risk worthwhile. This is often a matter of opinion and depends greatly on your goals and situation. If your goal is to make your first million by age forty and you're thirty-eight and barely worth $100,000, a daring risk with a fifty-fifty chance of failure but a potential million-dollar payoff might be acceptable. The same risk might not be acceptable if you're very close to that first million and don't need a long shot to pay off.

Questions to ask: What is my potential ROI in percentage terms? 300 percent? 400 percent? What are the odds that I will see such a return? In what time frame? How does this reward fit my goals?

— **RESEARCH AND PLANNING** means that once you decide the risk and reward are worthwhile, you educate yourself and create a strategy. In my business, research means finding out about the demographics of an area, its population growth trends, its economy, the value of comparable properties, and so on. Planning means that I develop a formula that I will follow from A to Z to achieve my goal. Charles and I provide just such a formula in the last chapter.

Questions to ask: What do I need to know to handle this risk properly? Where can I find the information? What steps should be included in my plan? Should I have someone review my plan to ensure I haven't forgotten anything?

— **PERSISTENT, CONSISTENT ACTION** means that once you jump into your risk, you don't stop working until you realize the reward, and you always act according to your plan. These are equally important. It's not hard to find people who do 80 percent of the work and then feel like they can coast the rest of the way. I have clients like that once in a while, people who get all the data, find an investment condo, and have all the paperwork in front of them, but won't do the last bit of work to reap the benefits. I don't know what they're waiting for.

You've also got to stick to your plan. It can be tempting to skip ahead five steps like you're playing a board game, but resist; you never know what you'll be missing if you decide, for example, not to check the zoning laws in a neighborhood before you invest in a preconstruction project. Maybe you would have found something that would prohibit the project and you could get out before you lose your deposit. Be methodical; who cares if other people call you "slow"? There's beauty in method.

Questions to ask: How much time will I have to commit to this goal? How many hours per day? What changes in my schedule will I have to make? What obstacles am I likely to encounter that will make me want to deviate from my plan?

That's a lot to keep in mind when you're in the middle of a risky situation. So it's good that we're going to talk about a productive "risk attitude" and how you can develop it. It's important because the fear of risk is crippling to our society.

LIVES OF QUIET DESPERATION

Henry David Thoreau said, "The mass of men lead lives of quiet desperation." Far too many of us spend our lives saying, "Tomorrow it will be different," and then doing nothing to change tomorrow. News flash: change doesn't just happen. You have to make it happen. Inertia is the epidemic of our age. People are unhappy with their jobs, their lives, their bodies, yet they take no action. Our society is filled with implicit warnings against opting out of the rat race. Instead, we're encouraged to buy more things with credit cards that we can't afford and probably don't need to numb the pain of knowing we're on a treadmill. According to CardWeb.com, the average American carries $9,312 in credit card debt, and according to Howard Dvorkin, founder of Consolidated Credit Counseling Services Inc., 65 percent of U.S. credit-card holders carry a balance on their cards from month to month, racking up millions in interest.

My, that was depressing, wasn't it? Well, it's true, unfortunately. Our conditioning to see risk as a source of fear, instead of seeing the uncertainty as a reason to strive and work and challenge ourselves, is debilitating. It's led to what I call the "cult of self-esteem." You know what I mean. The cult says that everyone deserves credit for just showing up and that everyone has equal value. It's a feel-good philosophy that attempts to level the playing field by rewarding mediocrity. Everyone does *not* have equal value. If you've spent the last ten years learning about buying and selling rural land to developers and now you're making a killing doing just that, you deserve more credit than the corporate drone who's spent years worrying about his retirement but never doing anything to ensure it.

Real self-esteem comes from putting it all on the line, working your tail off, getting up after you've taken a few shots to the chin, and making great things happen in the end. That's when you get to stand up when the dust clears and say, "Yeah! I did that!" I think it's wise to get into the habit of taking risks in your personal life so you learn how it feels to be uncertain, to not be good at something, and to fall on your face and get back up. Try public speaking, singing in front of an audience, running for local office, or taking a martial arts class. Do something that makes you a bit afraid. The fear of risk comes from the fear of uncertainty, of not being in control of all events. But if you can twist that fear around, you can turn uncertainty into a source of energy and power. And that's when you'll get off the treadmill and make real change happen in your life.

EMBRACING UNCERTAINTY CREATES ELECTRICITY

Human beings are a study in contradictions. On one hand, we spend much of our lives chasing safety: a home, a good job, a sense that we are prepared to weather the storms of life. But once we get there, do we have to stop growing? If you're reading this book it's likely you're in your twenties or thirties and maybe still pursuing that security. Maybe you're just out of graduate school, getting bored with your career choice, or trying for your first kid. Here's my advice: go for security in your personal life. Build a great family. Find a home you can cherish. Build a circle of friends you love and respect. Then start getting daring in your business life. You don't have to become fearful and conservative as you get older. Having a solid, secure personal foundation frees you to take big risks, shoot for the moon, and go out on a limb.

What we forget as we settle into routines is that all of life is risky. Risk and growth are tightly interwoven; babies cannot learn to walk until they first are willing to let go of the furniture and risk a fall. Then when they finally get the hang of it, what do they do? They flit from place to place like hummingbirds, bursting at the seams to take a new risk. Kids understand instinctively what we as adults—run by our rational, "responsible" minds—choose to ignore: if you want to grow, you must risk.

As adults, we convince ourselves that we're outsmarting risk and living in security. First of all, that's an illusion; there's precious little security anywhere these days. Second, there's risk all around us, every day. Our car could blow a tire on the highway at seventy-five miles per hour. The plane we're flying in could go down. Our company could go belly-up, or the stock market could crash and take our 401(k) with it. But as we make the mental bargain that if we don't notice the risk it doesn't exist, we blind ourselves to the power of risk to open our eyes to new possibilities. Companies that stop innovating and expanding into new markets become stagnant and find themselves bypassed by new, energetic upstarts, and adults who dig themselves a comfortable rut become inert.

Those amazing seniors we read about, the ninety-two-year-old water-skiing champions or eighty-eight-year-olds who climb mountains? Those are people who have continued to grow inside long after their biological growth has stopped because they have embraced the habit of smart risk taking. Wise risk keeps us—and our lives—more vital. The wildness and willingness to throw caution to the wind and leap into the unknown, so often associated with youth, are precisely what can make our lives really worth living.

When you read about high achievers, it's a good bet that when they were children their parents encouraged them to take smart risks and try new things—sports, auditioning for the school play—without fear of failure. In fact, the parents who best prepare their offspring to be risk takers teach their kids that if they fall short of a goal, they should get up, dust themselves off, and jump back in. These children learn the difference between smart risks and stupid ones and how to deal with both. A young person gains tremendous self-confidence by learning how to approach risk with wisdom and preparation and walk away a winner, which is why Outward Bound programs are so successful for troubled kids.

Uncertainty and risk are sources of power if you choose to see them that way. As with the rest of life, it's all in how you look at it. If you choose to view uncertainty as fearful, it will be. On the other hand, if you choose to view it as an opportunity, a period of time when the outcome is not guaranteed and you have the ability to influence events with your hard work, creativity, and smarts, then you'll find risk to be absolutely electrifying. That's the attitude you have to develop, a reflex that sees a potentially risky situation and, instead of first looking at how it could blow up in your face, first saying to yourself, "Where's the great opportunity here?" Because more often than not, there is an opportunity. Maybe more than one.

As a matter of fact, taking informed, wise risks becomes habit forming. When I decided I wanted to increase my risk tolerance, I became a serial house buyer. I buy properties like most women buy shoes. I love it. Each house I buy is an investment, but it's also a risk. I'm risking the property's having a hidden flaw, not being able to find a tenant, or choosing a tenant who doesn't pay his rent or causes damage. None of those things has happened yet, but any of them could tomorrow. But for me, the risk is a small consideration. First of all, the reward—the appreciation of my assets and building wealth—far outweighs the risk. And second, the risk makes me feel alive. It takes me out of my daily routine and pushes me to do a little bit better, a little bit more. It demands that I do my homework, make quick decisions, and plan for all contingencies. It's the same adrenaline rush that day traders get, probably the same thrill of nervous energy that actors and dancers and musicians get when the curtain goes up—you're putting it all on the line again and again and depending on your skill to make things come out all right.

RISK AND GROW RICH

"Risk and Grow Rich" means that you should go into risky situations fully aware, with plans and contingencies in place, knowing the odds and what you have to do to be successful. It's wise risk. You face risk practically every minute of every day, so why not embrace the risks rather than pretend they're not there? Accepting the idea that risk is not something to fear grants you power over it. People who step out of their comfort zone on a regular basis learn new skills, create opportunity where there was none, and inspire others to work with them. Risk takers are the only people in our society who are truly alive, every day. Daniel Kahneman, a pioneer of behavioral finance, shared the Nobel Prize for economics in 2002 for his research showing how humans' irrational behavior in the face of risk affects economic models. In short, people regularly fail to appreciate risk accurately—ignoring or failing to perceive major risks while overreacting to minor risks. Failure to understand what risk is can cripple your decision making.

THE THREE "ATES" THAT MAKE RISK PAY

If you think that I'm talking about chasing after the first wild hare that comes along or dumping everything you have into some crazy business scheme, stop right there. That's not what I mean. There is a word for people who take risks for risk's sake without any thought for the reward or the potential pitfalls: BROKE. I'm not counseling you to take stupid risks. Even if one pays off, it's going to be a matter of blind luck, not of your preparation and ability.

No, I'm talking about risks that can be governed by three core principles that I call the Three Ates. The Three Ates are the three things you must do to make a risk worthwhile. If an opportunity comes along and involves risk, look at it through these three principles. If they all apply, it might be worthwhile risk. If they don't, pass on it. These are the Three Ates:

— **CALCULATE.** You've heard of a "calculated risk" before. It means that before you jump into a risky venture, you determine the potential problems and the potential rewards, learn about the other people involved, anticipate possible obstacles and set up ways to deal with them, and so on. You plan and learn and become informed, and by doing so you reduce your risk.

Example: In December 2004, I was working with a condo conversion project in Miami called Vue at Brickell. The building was not even a year old, which is important because the older the building the higher the risk of structural problems. Now, this property is in downtown Miami—a hot, dynamic, fast-moving market. At this time it was not uncommon to open a project and have the entire building sell before construction even started. Demand was high and the developer was known for raising the prices substantially. I was able to get my buyers in at a price they would have gotten if they had been locals. There was great potential that they would close with a substantial amount of equity. Of course, there were potential problems. A lot of people were skeptical because there was a lot of construction in the area, so there was a glut of inventory. People were afraid to buy because they wouldn't have the equity they thought they did. My clients and I evaluated their risks. Potential problem: they couldn't resell their unit. Potential problem: they would have to put down more money out of pocket. They would be paying about $465,000, which in that area at that time was a high price. Potential problem: they might not have been able to rent the place. Part of Calculate is becoming informed. I urged my clients to study the area's job growth, economy, and real estate market.

— **INITIATE.** Once you're informed and prepared and have decided the risk is a good one, act first and act fast. Force the action. Take control by being decisive and being a catalyst for other people. Be consistent in your actions and never, ever quit. Persistence is one of the most underrated qualities in successful risk taking, but when you think about it, it's invaluable. How many billion-dollar companies wouldn't exist right now if their founders had quit when the risk got a little too hairy?

Example: Once my clients were informed, they had to make a quick decision. In real estate in Florida, when you buy a new condo, you have a fifteen-day recision period when you can sign a contract, change your mind, and get your deposit back without penalty. What I tell my clients to do is become as informed as they can as quickly as they can, but if they trust their gut and they trust me, then jump in. Act fast. Write the contract, do the deal, then finish becoming informed within the fifteen days. If the deal doesn't look good, back out. Many clients want to sleep on it, and by the time they decide to do the deal all the units are sold. Make the rules work for you. These clients did and they bought.

— **MITIGATE.** This is one you won't find anywhere else. Mitigate means that before you dive into the risky situation, look for ways that you can benefit even if it doesn't pay off, because not all calculated risks pay off. Sometimes people drop the ball. Other times, you misjudge or just get plain unlucky. By mitigating, you might see some key business contacts you can make as a result of the opportunity; you might see another opportunity that could grow out of the first one; or there might be a new skill you could learn that you couldn't get anywhere else. Mitigation not only allows you to take something away from a risk that falls flat, but it helps you see and take advantage of those extra benefits that are there even if things do work out.

Example: If my clients had decided they didn't want to do the deal in the fifteen days, at least they would have educated themselves. Every time you evaluate a property, you learn something. You're more informed for the next time. My clients learned about the local market, demographics, economic statistics, and more.

With the Three Ates, you'll be well-prepared for taking risk, and you'll be able to recognize a stupid risk from one with the potential to take you to new heights of success. When you're ready, I'd suggest writing the Ates down and when you run across an opportunity that also represents a substantial risk, apply the Ates to it. When you calculate the risk and reward, does it make sense to go ahead with it? Do you have the ability to take the initiative and drive the action? Are you dependent on someone else, or worse, on chance? And are there mitigating factors that will salvage the venture if the risk doesn't pay off? Based on the answers to those questions, you'll know what to do.

In the Vue at Brickell deal, my clients took the risk and did very well. If you want the higher payoff, you have to do the bigger deals. People tend to focus on the negative: the possibility of not finding a renter, higher carrying costs (mortgage, insurance), and the like. The higher price the property, the more they focus on the negative and not the reward. But if you recognize that a more expensive property will yield a bigger payoff, you should do the deal. These people did just that. And you know what? I ran into them at a real estate show in San Diego a year later and their condo had already appreciated $160,000. They were out of pocket $46,500 for a down payment, then $10,000 in closing costs. They found a renter within two months and they were renting the place for at least $1,600 a month. They knew they were going to have negative cash flow but they didn't worry about it. Why? They had done their research. They knew what I knew: in 2001, the Miami market had appreciated over 50%. They knew they were going to get some serious equity. They were only negative $200 a month, $2,400 a year, which means the rent didn't cover all their costs, such as homeowner's association fees and insurance. But they have been able to carry that extra cost with ease, and they've made many times that in appreciation. You can't tell me that making $160K in equity in only a year isn't worth a little negative cash flow. When they sell, even if they pay capital gains taxes and commission, they stand to earn as much as 100 times that annual carrying cost, depending on when they sell and how much the property has increased in value.

We'll talk in detail about how to make use of that kind of home equity in chapter 9, "A Formula for Making Your First Million."

FAMOUS RISK TAKERS

Every great human endeavor involves risk. It's impossible to escape. If you want proof, take a look at this short list of some great people who became great only because they were willing to stick their necks out for a vision they believed in:

— **THOMAS ALVA EDISON.** This quintessential American genius was near starvation three weeks after arriving in New York. Wandering through the financial district, he discovered that the stock ticker at an important brokerage had failed. Edison repaired it in seconds, landed a job with the brokerage, and used that security to begin cranking out inventions that have made the modern world possible—the incandescent lightbulb; the world's first central system for distributing heat, light, and power; the storage battery; the Dictaphone; and what would become the motion picture camera. In all, Edison holds an astonishing 1,093 patents.

— **ERIN BROCKOVICH.** This tough-minded mother of three risked a desperately needed job to initiate the largest direct action lawsuit of its kind at the time against Pacific Gas & Electric. The settlement, the largest toxic tort settlement in history, turned Brockovich into a heroine of the underdog and her story into an Oscar-winning movie. She went from broke to wealthy and famous and continues to crusade for the underdog in class action lawsuits against the likes of Avon Corporation.

— **HOWARD SCHULZ.** This son of a diaper delivery driver grew up in subsidized housing in Brooklyn and envisioned building a global brand that would not only become profitable but help alleviate poverty. He did it with little or no advertising, simply because the company couldn't afford it. So he set out to build a bond of trust with his employees and to do good around the world, such as contributing to farming projects in Ethiopia. The result? More than 3,500 Starbucks across the globe, over 50,000 employees (called "partners"), and ownership of, among other properties, the NBA's Seattle Supersonics.

— **BUGSY SIEGEL.** He saw "Las Vegas" where 99 percent of others saw only scorched Nevada desert. Billions of gamblers later, he's seen as a visionary.

— **KATHARINE HEPBURN.** Astonishingly written off as box office poison in 1938, Hepburn was determined to regain her star status, so she bought the film rights to the Broadway play *The Philadelphia Story,* a role written for her by Philip Barry. Hepburn's risk paid off: when MGM wanted to make the hit into a film, they not only had to cast her, but also give her veto power over the director and cast. The film was a smash, winning an Oscar for costar Jimmy Stewart and putting Hepburn back atop the heap.

— **RICHARD BRANSON.** This brash British mogul might be best known these days for his round-the-world balloon adventures. But before all that, he was the founder of Virgin Records and the author of an audacious plan: to launch an upstart airline that would compete with mammoth British Airways. Critics told him he would lose everything, and in true risk-taker fashion, he went ahead anyway. Today, Virgin Atlantic Airways is the second-largest airline in Britain, and is the foundation for the Branson empire that includes financial, retail, music, Internet, rail, hotels, cola, and now even Virgin Galactic, the world's first space tourism company.

— **MARY KAY ASH.** This former saleswoman decided to help women thrive in a male-dominated business world. In 1963, with $5,000, she started Mary Kay Cosmetics. Today, her company is global and she and her pink Cadillacs for her top salespeople are an icon.

— **STEVE JOBS.** After cofounding Apple Computer with Steve Wozniak in 1976, Jobs helped to create the personal computing market with the release of the Apple II and the Macintosh. Leaving the company to found Pixar, NeXT, and other successful enterprises, he came back to run the company in 1996. Risking very public failure, he helped to revive the sagging company with products like the iMac and wildly successful iPod. Today, Apple is a global behemoth brand and Jobs's net worth is in the $3 billion range.

— **WALTER O'MALLEY.** The long-time owner of the Brooklyn Dodgers had a recent championship and an adoring fan base in 1957, but he also had a small, run-down stadium in Ebbets Field and a city that refused to let him build the new stadium he needed to continue to draw the team's fans, who were flocking to the new suburbs on Long Island. So, despite a rancorous fan outcry and the risk that West Coast fans would not embrace his transplant team, O'Malley convinced the Giants to leave Manhattan and relocate to California along with the Dodgers for the 1958 season. He even got prime land from the city of Los Angeles. The result: a sports franchise valued today at about $425 million, behind only the Yankees, Boston Red Sox, and New York Mets.

> **"The more you seek security, the less of it you have. But the more you seek opportunity, the more likely it is that you will achieve the security that you desire."**
>
> **Brian Tracy, speaker, consultant, and author of more than thirty books on business and personal success**

These are all extraordinary people, you say? Sure they are—now. But all extraordinary people start out as ordinary people who find the courage to undertake great risks and persist against long odds. They were once as ordinary as any man on the street. It's your actions that define you, not any sense of destiny or greatness. In Shakespeare's comedy *Twelfth Night*, Sir Toby Belch and his friends make fun of the pompous Malvolio by sending him a fake love letter that includes the famous lines, "Some are born great, some achieve greatness, and some have greatness thrust upon them." I think only the middle claim is true: greatness is a choice to go over the edge with both eyes open and try to make great things happen.

WHAT KIND OF RISK TAKER ARE YOU?

What kind of risk taker are you? What kind do you want to become? There's a way to find out. I've developed a test to discover what I call your Risk Index. Answer the following questions honestly and tally up your score at the end to get a picture of the type of business and financial risk taker you are shaping up to be.

RISK INDEX TEST

1. When confronted with a situation that might involve immediate risk, your reflex response is to:

> (a) Get your adrenaline pumping and jump in immediately.

> (b) Assess the situation and look for the opportunities.

> (c) Look for ways to avoid the situation.

> (d) Become afraid and retreat immediately to a comfort zone.

2. When the potential risk is in the distant future, such as an investment in a development that's a year from completion, how do you prepare?

> (a) You don't. You wing it and trust your abilities.

> (b) You make bold, aggressive plans to take full advantage of any opportunities.

(c) You do nothing, worry about it, then prepare in haste at the eleventh hour.

(d) You do nothing, become more panicked, then try to back out at the last minute.

3. When a risky situation ends in failure, how do you explain it to yourself?

(a) You determine that you didn't act aggressively enough.

(b) You chalk it up to "stuff happens." You figure out what you can learn and look for your next opportunity.

(c) You blame others.

(d) You blame your own failings and resolve never to take *that* risk again.

4. How often have you deliberately done something that's been far outside your comfort zone, just for the sake of expanding your abilities or conquering your fear?

(a) On a regular basis.

(b) Once in a while, when the mood takes me.

(c) Rarely.

(d) Never.

5. When others tell you your risk is "crazy," what is your response?

(a) You rise to the challenge and try to "sell" them on your risk.

(b) If they have sound reasons, you listen and assess. If they don't, you ignore them and keep preparing.

(c) You begin to doubt your ability or preparation.

(d) You abandon your plans.

6. When all the information comes together to show that a risky opportunity is sound, how do you react?

(a) You jump in without hesitation.

(b) You double check your facts and figures, then act.

(c) You ask others what you should do.

(d) You do nothing.

7. How does being on your own in a risky situation make you feel?

(a) Challenged and stimulated.

(b) Confident.

(c) Uncertain but hopeful.

(d) Frightened.

8. If you encountered a real estate opportunity that looked great but you lacked the cash, what would you do?

(a) Take out a second mortgage on your house.

(b) Borrow from friends or relatives.

(c) Hope that the opportunity would keep while trying to save the money.

(d) Figure it's not meant to be.

9. If you were convinced a colleague's business idea was fantastic but were unsure about his ability to manage a company, would you invest venture capital in his company?

(a) Yes.

(b) Yes, but only if you had the power to approve or veto management decisions.

(c) Yes, but not until he had operated profitably for one year.

(d) No.

10. When a risk pays off, how do you feel?

(a) Unstoppable.

(b) Vindicated.

(c) Relieved.

(d) Surprised.

Scoring

Write down your answers and give yourself four points for every (a), three for every (b), two for every (c), and one point for every (d). Then add up your points, and rate yourself as a risk taker according to this scale:

35–40 points: You're a "Cowboy," probably too ready to jump into risks without proper preparation. You might get some pay-offs, but you'll probably lose as often as you win. You thrive on a steady diet of adrenaline. You need to learn to say "Whoa!" and add some caution and due diligence to the mix.

27–34 points: You're "Risk Certain," someone who's bold but not reckless, with the right balance of aggression and rational planning.

18–26 points: You're "Risk Uncertain," someone who straddles the fence on risky situations, sometimes jumping in, sometimes running away.

10–17 points: You're "Risk Averse," someone who retreats from risk if given the slightest opportunity. You're very happy in your comfort zone and will stay there if given the chance.

1–9 points: You're a "Monk," terrified of risk and interested only in the predictable and the guaranteed. Risk paralyzes you and you never step outside your comfort zone for any reason. You need to hop the monastery wall, get out into the world, and check out the amazing opportunities all around you.

Guess which one of these five I'd like to see you become? If you said Risk Certain, good call. Being Risk Certain means you have no fear of risks, but you assess business or personal risks rationally and factually, walking away from those in which the negatives outweigh the positives. You might choose to skydive for the adrenaline rush, but if the instructor seems unprofessional, you'll back out because the risk of dying due to lack of proper preparation far outweighs the potential of fun.

You can almost always see a direct relationship between your Risk Index and the life you're leading today. Do you tend to adhere to the conventional wisdom? Are you in the same career your mother or father was in? Have you missed business or investment opportunities that turned out to have huge payoffs? You're probably Risk Averse or a Monk. Have you taken big chances and gotten burned, such as making investments based on a handshake or gambling with your life savings? You're a Cowboy, and you're probably living paycheck to paycheck. Your attitude toward risk determines your lifestyle and, very often, how happy you are with that lifestyle.

But here's the good news: you can change your Risk Index. It's a snapshot of where you are now. It doesn't have to be where you are in five years. Every time you take a step outside your comfort zone or back off from a foolhardy risk to plan and prepare, you adjust your Risk Index and bring it closer to that 27–34 sweet spot where the sharp entrepreneurs, savvy investors, and mountain climbers of the world live. After you read this book, start keeping track of the things you do that take you outside your comfort zone. Write them down, then in a year look at your list and retake the Risk Index Test. If you've taken deliberate steps to take more, smarter risks, you'll see your score improve. Then you're on your way!

ARE YOU RISKING ENOUGH TO BE RICH?

I don't consider myself an extraordinary person. But I feel I was fortunate because my mother and father were always telling me that I could do anything. By the time I went to high school in Virginia, it was ingrained in my personality: I could succeed at anything. That's why I was always trying something new, from sports to art. Because of my upbringing and the confidence my parents instilled in me, I was never shy or afraid. I've never been the kind of person who says, "I can't do that." It's just not in my nature.

Because of my natural ability to take risks, things have happened in my life that I consider pretty extraordinary. If I hadn't had a long history of taking smart risks, I might still have a great life, but I would have missed out on a lot of amazing things and people that have come into my life because of good risk taking.

That's the real tragedy of being afraid of risk. You'll never know what you missed by staying on the sidelines. That's why I began this book with the quote from my favorite Robert Frost poem. When you take the well-traveled road, you'll never know what you could have accomplished had you jumped into the uncertainty and gone after what you want even though it made you nervous and scared. But when you take the road less traveled and reach some amazing goal, you can stop, look back, and see what your life would have been like if you'd refused the risk. You'd be exactly where you were those weeks, months, or years before. Whether or not that would be a good thing is up to you, but I don't know too many people who would rather be less excited about their jobs, less wealthy, or have fewer opportunities.

The question to ask yourself as we begin this journey together is, are you taking enough risks to feel energized, challenged, and fully alive? That's really the goal. You don't need to get rich in real estate or get on a TV show to have risks pay off. You just need to feel like you're fully living your life the way you want to. There's no formula.

I'm going to help you train yourself to respond in a different way to risk than you may have in the past. There are two distinct schools of what I call "comfort zone violation response," that is, how people respond when confronted with something that's outside their comfort zone, from scuba diving to buying stock:

Loser Response

Responds to possible risk with:

— Fear

— Self-doubt

— Excuses

— Worry

Winner Response

Responds to possible risk with:

— Insatiable curiosity

— Sense of challenge

— Planning

— Passion

I'm going to go out on a limb here and guess that you'd rather not be a loser. So it's time to start changing the way you react to the idea of something that takes you out of your comfort zone. If your automatic pilot tells you to decline the invitation to dive or invest or sing in front of a crowd, ask yourself, "Why?" What are you missing out on by passing on those chances to step into the danger zone just a little?

Because that's what really does separate ordinary lives from extraordinary lives: the readiness to look at risks clearly, assess the rewards and hazards, do wise planning, then jump in and swim for all you're worth. That approach to risk is what creates *Fortune* 500 corporations, great works of art, and world-changing organizations like Habitat for Humanity. Extraordinary people take extraordinary risks as a matter of daily practice. They're not reckless, but they are unafraid. Lance Armstrong risked his reputation, his pride, and his health when he jumped back on his bike after beating cancer to compete in the Tour de France. Now, after seven wins in a row, he's a world-class hero and a model for overcoming seemingly insurmountable obstacles.

Are you taking enough risks to have the extraordinary wealth that you've always seen for yourself? By taking smart risks, you provoke results. You force the action. You make people take notice of you. Taking an intelligent risk is taking control, refusing to be at the mercy of an employer, government, or economy. And when your risk pays off, you'll never feel more powerful—until the next one hits the jackpot. Then you're hooked.

Now, let's move ahead and take a look at something very important: the most common myths about risk and why they are simply not true.

2.

THE TEN BIGGEST MYTHS ABOUT RISK

Chance favors the prepared mind.

LOUIS PASTEUR, LECTURE, UNIVERSITY OF LILLE

Successful risk takers sometimes end up being larger than life—the Mercury astronauts, for example, or casino and hotel magnate Steve Wynn—so it's not surprising that plenty of myths spring up about risk and risk takers. Listen to the myths and you'd think that all great risk takers were millionaire adventurers with gazes of steel and steady hands, daredevils who push the envelope and live on the edge twenty-four hours a day. No wonder the idea of stepping outside your comfort zone can be intimidating with role models like those!

Of course, myths are completely false at worst and not necessarily true at best. Sure, there are some successful risk takers who are titans of industry or culture, who are world famous, who are cultural icons defying the laws that seem to apply to someone else. But here's a little something you may not realize: those so-called titans are no different from you. Neither are the millions of other successful risk takers you've never heard of. There's nothing special about them—except an ability to get up every morning without the fear of making mistakes or failure and stride boldly into high-risk, high-reward situations with the proper preparation, rolling with the punches and accepting any setbacks not as failures, but as lessons.

There is nothing about triumphant risk takers—the entrepreneurs, artists, and leaders you admire—that you don't have within yourself. You just need to find it and coax it to the surface. But first, you need to see the myths about risk for what they are: lies concocted by those who fear risk to make themselves feel better about their failures.

Once you see through the myths, you'll see there's nothing about great risk takers that you cannot emulate. So let's burst some bubbles and shatter some preconceptions, shall we?

Myth 1: Risk is bad.
Truth: Risk is essential.

You could say this is the granddaddy of them all, the idea that risk is automatically something to fear. We've had the idea drilled into our heads by insurance companies who hire actuaries to gauge likely risk, financial planners who talk about risk as a dirty word, and round-the-clock news channels that bring us the gruesome highlights of every mountain climbing, river rafting, and extreme racing mishap. In short, we're conditioned to think of risk as something scary, something to be avoided at all costs.

The result of this narrow thinking is that we've become a society of good little foot soldiers who are content to hunker down in our self-made risk bunkers, focused on our lives as they are, without the thought even entering our minds to poke our heads over the tops of our cubicles to see what our lives *could be.* Are you one of the drones on whom the wealth and power of our society is built, the ones who never question, who never step out of line? Do you identify with the soulless, absurdist workplace in the movie *Office Space,* where TPS reports are everything and birthday celebrations have all the enthusiasm of a line at the Department of Motor Vehicles?

To make the picture as clear as possible, I'm going to cite one of Kendra's Rules of Risk, one that illustrates the hazards of living a life without risk in a way you may never have considered:

KENDRA'S RULE OF RISK 1

Those who will not risk end up producing wealth for others rather than themselves.

This isn't to say that all corporations are risk averse or stunt the growth of their people: you can look at Toyota and its visionary release of the Prius hybrid vehicle, or 3M and its policy that encourages its research and development people to spend some of their time on their own projects, sparking innovation. These companies have embraced risk as a business strategy and reaped the rewards—witness Toyota's stock price versus Ford's or GM's.

But it's more common to see organizations that fear risk, from the CEO's corner office all the way down to the employee lunchroom. Top executives shun risk, worried they might jeopardize their stock price or golden parachute or even their job, and as a result they infect the whole enterprise with fear. Rank-and-file employees who, with a little encouragement, might discover their entrepreneurial side, and with creativity and bold thinking breathe life back into the corporation, learn by example that risk will not be tolerated. As a result, most will fail to develop their abilities to the fullest, while their companies stagnate, miss opportunities, and squander their ability to compete. Everybody loses—companies fail, thousands of now-out-of-work would-be entrepreneurs never learn to take the risks that would give them control over what they do and what they earn, and the only ones getting rich are the executives who walk away with obscene severance packages.

Let me present an alternative to the idea that risk is bad: *not taking risks is bad.* From a career perspective, taking wise, calculated risks gives you control. If you start your own company, strike out on your own as a freelancer, or become an independent investor, you are the captain of your own vessel for better or worse. If the economy shifts, you're still affected by it, but you make the decisions on how to deal with the rough seas, not some boss who has his own agenda that does not include what's best for you! You're more in charge of your fate when you're willing to risk.

Can risk be bad? Of course. Reckless, poorly planned, or self-destructive risks can be catastrophic. Even seemingly smart risk takers, like the fifteen Everest climbers who lost their lives on May 10, 1996, in the disaster chronicled in John Krakauer's *Into Thin Air,* can be overtaken by unfortunate circumstances that turn questionable judgment into life-or-death decisions. But for the most part, wise risks give you power and control. That's nothing but good.

EXAMPLE: When three friends and I started *Capture Life* magazine, we were four recent college graduates who didn't know anything about the magazine industry. We learned everything on the fly, as we did it, learning how to put together a magazine by looking at competing magazines. When we launched in 2001, we had $100,000 in startup capital raised from the father of one of the partners. With all the capital expenses we had in starting the business— office space, marketing, distribution, equipment—we only made $34,000 back in advertising with the first issue, so we were already $66,000 in the red before the first issue went on sale. Yet because I learned everything that goes into creating a business, it was one of the most valuable risks I ever took.

Myth 2: Risk takers can't afford to make mistakes. Truth: Making mistakes is the way risk takers learn.

This one is completely ridiculous, as most of the wealthiest, most successful people in the world have experienced one or more catastrophic failures in their lives. As the great jazz saxophonist Ornette Coleman said, "It was when I found out I could make mistakes that I knew I was on to something." For Coleman, "mistakes" equaled breaking free of what he called the "caste system" of sound and riding the wave of "compositional inspiration" that had allowed jazz—particularly bebop—to break free of conventional structure and become a truly unique form of expression. Ask any successful person—by definition someone who has mastered the art of smart risk taking—about the value of mistakes and he or she will no doubt say that mistakes were the source of his or her greatest inspiration.

If you are not making mistakes, you are not taking enough risks. Risk gives off error as a by-product like internal combustion gives off carbon monoxide. Think about it: if you're not making any mistakes, then you're firmly in your comfort zone, where you know your skill set is sufficient, you can predict what's to come with reasonable accuracy, and you have little apprehension. You're in a rut. That's not security. That's stagnation.

Mistakes are the most powerful sources of new insight and self-knowledge a risk taker possesses. Successful individuals will often talk about "making mistakes well" or "making loud mistakes." Behind those phrases is a powerful idea that many people who are stuck in their comfort zone never even contemplate: if you're going to make mistakes, make bold, big, productive ones that upset the status quo, reveal people's character, and uncover new ways of doing things that you can try next time. Most important, make mistakes that show you how *not* to do something, so you can correct yourself the next time around. The things you do right do little for your growth; in fact, they often give you a false sense of confidence. But doing things wrong humbles you and shows you what you still need to learn, how hard you still need to work, how far you still must travel to become the person you aspire to be.

Big mistakes can be your Yoda, Buddha, and favorite college professor rolled into one. They are the greatest teachers you will ever have. As Daniel C. Dennett, Director of the Center for Cognitive Studies at Tufts University, says, "Instead of shunning mistakes . . . you should cultivate the habit of making them. Instead of turning away in denial when you make a mistake, you should become a connoisseur of your own mistakes, turning them over in your mind as if they were works of art, which in a way they are. You should seek out opportunities to make grand mistakes, just so you can then recover from them."

The one thing a risk taker should never do with mistakes, however, is be intimidated into inaction by them. As Winston Churchill once said, "Success is the ability to go from failure to failure without losing your enthusiasm." You are going to fail. You are going to misjudge, be ill prepared, and suffer from bad luck or a bad choice of partners. It happens, so get over it, look at the reasons why you made the mistakes you did, correct them, and move on to make new mistakes.

KENDRA'S RULE OF RISK 2

If you are not making mistakes, you are not taking sufficient risk.

If you want to bring transformation and new opportunity into your life, you've got to overcome your fear of mistakes and start embracing the idea of error. Jump in with both feet. Swim. So what if you're slow or you swim the wrong way? Plenty of people never even get their feet wet. Eventually, you'll find your bearings.

EXAMPLE: When I first got into the real estate business, I made the mistake of giving my price sheet to a client. When they came back to look at a project I had been trying to sell them on and saw that the prices had gone up, they were angry. It was embarrassing, but it helped me to refine my process. Now I always give people a disclaimer and let people know that prices are always changing and any numbers I give them are strictly temporary. I don't make the mistake of tainting their expectations by giving them price information they might assume is set in stone. Mistakes help you refine your process. I've learned more about this business from my mistakes than I ever will from my successful deals.

Myth 3: Risk takers are fearless.
Truth: Risk takers feel fear but don't let it control them.

Notice that I didn't say you had to lose your fear of mistakes; you just have to overcome it. Fear is natural, and there's not a risk taker out there who doesn't feel fear at one time or another. Some feel fear all the time. If you're climbing Everest, fear can keep you alive. Fear prevents you from taking stupid risks or from letting your emotions overrule your common sense and make you do things you not only know are dangerous but that you are ill prepared for. Only fools feel no fear.

My father, John Todd, was a Navy fighter pilot. But he wasn't just any old Navy pilot; he was one of the best in the world, an instructor at Top Gun in Miramar, California. He was the one who instilled in me the idea that going after what you want and taking risks is noble. He was a Civil War enthusiast and used to take me to battlefields all around the South—Manassas, Chancellorsville, and others. His words brought those battles to life for me: men on both sides marching in lines toward rifle fire, knowing they were likely to die and doing it anyway, risking everything for causes they believed in. Dad shaped my whole vision of risk and sacrifice.

In fact, one of my clearest memories of the nobility of risk came when my father and I were watching a History Channel show about World War II. An image of a ship came on and my dad jumped out of his chair and said, "That's your grandfather's ship!" The video showed the ship being hit by a kamikaze plane, and Dad told me the story of how my grandfather, having survived the impact, had to choose between jumping off the burning ship into shark-infested waters or hanging from the railing hoping for rescue before the flames overcame him. My grandfather chose to hang on and was rescued, and that story had an enormous effect on me. I saw that fear didn't have to prevent sound judgment.

In fact, my father told me that when he flew, he was almost always afraid for his life. He had to make night landings on aircraft carriers in the

Indian Ocean. Any former Navy pilot you talk to will tell you there's nothing more unnerving than a nighttime carrier landing, when the flight deck is bobbing and weaving like a drunk on the swells and the lights that mark home and safety are tiny specks on a vast dark sea. He was always afraid during those landings, he confessed. Any sane man would be. But he never let his fear interfere with what he had to do. He controlled the fear; he didn't let it control him.

Chances are, you'll never take a risk as hair-raising as a night carrier landing. That doesn't mean you won't feel fear. And that's okay. Fear is your brain telling you to exercise caution, to keep your eyes open, and to plan for the worst while hoping for the best. The opposite of fear isn't courage but recklessness. If you pay attention to your fear and listen to what it's trying to tell you about the risk you're considering, you'll act with care and not make foolish, reckless mistakes. Just don't let your fear drive your actions and make you retreat from risks. That's panic. Panic is the emotion that drives out thought. Learn to know the difference between prudent fear and blind panic. Then banish panic from your mind.

EXAMPLE: Right before I sign a contract on a piece of real estate as a personal investment, I am always nervous. I see people manage risk every day and I still get nervous, even though I'm one of the most informed people in the industry. That's just being human; any time you approach a big risk, you're going to have butterflies in your stomach. Anyone who says otherwise is lying. Not long ago, I bought a condo on the Intracoastal Waterway in a community called Yacht Club on the Intracoastal. For those who don't know the Intracoastal, it's a connected network of canals, inlets, and protected waterways that runs down much of the southeastern coast of the United States. It's also some of the most coveted residential property in the region. I bought this unit for $315,000, which at that time was the most expensive property I had bought. I knew that the developer had a history of aggressive price increases. I didn't even make my real estate commission on the deal; I sacrificed it because I was so eager to get the deal done. I was very nervous, because I was going against my own formula of sticking to a recession-proof price point. I was buying at the top of the market instead. Fortunately, I conquered my fears and went ahead with the deal. On the day my property closed, the unit next to mine sold for $405,000. So I had $90,000 of equity at closing, and I've made a lot more since. As long as I can rent properties like this one, I hold them and let them appreciate, taking out equity lines on each one that I don't use until I need to. In the Florida market, I'm building valuable equity that I use to constantly expand my holdings. Of course, owning the property also gives you the option of cashing out when you need to or when you feel the market has peaked, walking away with a tidy profit. We'll talk more about the uses of equity in chapter 9.

Myth 4: Risk takers are overnight successes.
Truth: Becoming a smart, brave risk taker can take years of learning.

This one always cracks me up. I hear it myself on occasion when someone asks me, "So, Kendra, what's it like to be an overnight success?" I want to tell the person, hey, this overnight success was twenty years in the making, all right? The groundwork for the success I'm enjoying today was laid when I was a kid, then in high school, then in college, then in my hard but rewarding times running a magazine, *Capture Life*, that I started with friends when I was fresh out of college and couldn't get a job. Running on a shoestring budget, the magazine became a successful, thriving enterprise, but it took long hours of demanding work that was not very financially rewarding (more about this in the next chapter). So there really are no overnight successes, just people who have been working long and hard whose achievements are just now drawing some attention.

Success never happens quickly. Remember those mistakes I was talking about, the ones so many captains of industry and geniuses of the arts have made? They take time. But it is the nature of public perception to be attracted only to the victorious and the glamorous, so 99 percent of risk takers remain invisible until they have made their fortune, won their Oscar, or moved into the CEO's office. The public never sees—nor does it want to see—the hard work, mistakes, failures, sacrifices, and self-doubts that led to the wealth and fame they celebrate.

But as a risk taker in training, it's important that you avoid buying into the concept of overnight success. If you do, you're likely to be discouraged by the slow pace of progress toward your ultimate goal and by the failures that are sure to litter your path along the way. But we as Americans have been brainwashed by Hollywood into believing that success can come out of nowhere like a lightning strike: the starlet discovered in the coffee shop, the inventor who changes the world and becomes a millionaire overnight. In this age of the glorification of wealth, we're told we should all be aspiring to be instantly rich rappers or NBA all-stars. Our popular culture sells us the dream that success is easy and comes overnight to those who deserve it, and we buy the dream. But it's a lie.

It doesn't matter how great a risk you take, you can't fight the fact that success takes time. Even those who are supremely talented and jump into professional sports or music years before their peers take time to blossom. How many young basketball players did you hear about who entered the NBA right out of high school (a practice the league has wisely ended in its new collective bargaining agreement), their eyes filled with dreams and dollar signs, only to disappear? Jazz chanteuse Norah Jones seemed to burst onto the music scene at age twenty-two in 2002 with her Grammy-winning album *Come Away With Me,* but in reality that was only the culmination of years of working on her songwriting, vocal technique, and performing, work that began when she played her first gig at The Living Room, a coffeehouse on Manhattan's Lower East Side, at age sixteen. Thomas Edison may have developed the carbonized filament that enabled the early lightbulb to last and provide reliable illumination, but he tried and failed first with such materials as platinum and spent a year designing the other key components behind a reliable bulb such as a high-efficiency vacuum pump. Behind every so-called overnight success lies a long back story.

I have a formula for debunking the myth of overnight success. The next time you encounter someone new and hot on the scene, whether it's an actor or a businessperson, take the amount of time you've been hearing about that person and multiply it by five. That's at least how long that individual has been working, risking, and climbing to reach the top, only you didn't know about it.

Does that make you feel better? It should. The fact that overnight success is a fantasy should give you hope that you can take your own risks and reach your goals without feeling the pressure to get there in weeks or months. It takes years. Enjoy the ride. Meet people. Learn and gain wisdom. When you do finally get to your goal, the sweat you've put in and the perspective you've gained will make you appreciate it even more.

EXAMPLE: I get up early and I work late, I sacrifice weekends, and I sacrifice going home to see my family during the holidays because my business takes a lot of work. If you talk to people who have made millions in real estate, they'll all tell you the same thing: the first million is the hardest. That first million was not made with one real estate transaction. It's like Monopoly: you go from little houses to hotels, then to a multimillion-dollar portfolio. One client of ours, Gary, worked hard for years to build up a real estate portfolio so his family would be taken care of when he was gone. His first property was a run-down little duplex in a low-end neighborhood, but he bought it for what it was: a stepping stone. Over the years, he and his wife bought more and more and increased their cash flow, using the equity from their past investments to catapult themselves into bigger deals. After a while they were doing million-dollar deals. It didn't happen overnight; it took years of dedicated work. Truly big scores come along once in a blue moon; making money takes relentless work. Well, Gary passed away not too long ago, and because of his wise investments, his family is well taken care of.

Myth 5: Risk takers are born, not made.
Truth: You can train yourself to embrace risk.

No wonder some folks feel you have to be born rich to risk. With adventurers like Steve Fossett and Richard Branson ballooning around the world and launching rockets into space while appearing all over our TVs, it's no wonder many believe that risk is something reserved for billionaires with too much time on their hands.

Hogwash. This is an excuse for people who are afraid to stick their necks out and take a risk for fear of failure. They say, "But I'm just not made that way." That's garbage. There is no genetic imprint that makes some people risk takers and other people timid guardians of the status quo. Risk taking is a learned behavior. Risk takers are made, not born.

In my work in real estate and in starting my magazine, I responded to risks according to my temperament and upbringing. That's one of the key principles you need to understand: your ability and willingness to risk depends on who you are as a complete person, not just on your aggressiveness, your emotions, your threshold for danger, or anything else. I didn't develop my tendency to dare risks deliberately; it was a natural outgrowth of my upbringing, when my parents drilled it into my head that there was nothing I couldn't do. I learned early on to dare and risk and strive and fail and get up and start all over again. That has everything to do with how I approach risk today.

Of course, if you're reading this, it's probably a little too late for you to train yourself to embrace risk from childhood. That's okay. You don't have to learn it as a child, as long as you learn it. You can retrain yourself to love risk rather than fear it, to see the possibility in risk/reward situations instead of the chance of disaster. If you respond to risky situations according to your character, and you don't like how you respond, it's time to modify your character and retune your risk profile!

Easy for me to say, but changing how you face risk is a matter of habit and repetition. There are three things you should be doing consistently to elevate your risk threshold:

1. **Find a new explanation for failure.** When things go wrong, people who are afraid of risk blame themselves for things that are beyond their control, turn their own mistakes into self-indictments of their character or abilities, and convince themselves that they will never be

able to improve. Wise risk takers accept their own errors but know they are temporary and can be corrected, recognize external factors for what they are, and are always determined to try again.

2. **Start taking small risks.** Dip your toe in the water and do small things that take you out of your comfort zone, such as introducing yourself to strangers or joining a new social circle, whether it's a church club or ski group. You'll be as comfortable as a pig on roller skates at first, but you'll soon discover two things: the discomfort isn't fatal, and you'll feel great that you had the courage to step out of your rut. That's one thing no one tells you about a successful risk—it's an incredible high! Once you get used to small risks, take larger ones, then larger ones.

3. **Hang out with risk takers.** If you make friends of people who are always pushing the boundaries and trying new things, you'll learn the language of risk takers. You'll be inspired. You'll see they're not very different from you, they just have a different outlook on life. They look at it as a gourmet meal waiting to be devoured, where maybe you've looked at it until now as unappetizing cafeteria food. Take a seat at the table and dig in.

You can remake your nature. You can train yourself not only to embrace risk when you find it, but eventually to seek it out and create your own risk to change your life, your income, and your future. Once you get past the idea that only certain kinds of individuals are born to take risks, everything else becomes possible.

EXAMPLE: If you're not making money with your friends, get new friends. One of the best ways to make yourself into a successful risk taker is to associate with people who have already turned risk into wealth. When I'm talking to a thirty-four-year-old developer who's made millions, I'm one step closer to the ideas that generated those millions. When you put successful people on a pedestal, they become remote. They're just people. Charles and I are lucky enough to work with a company called SunVest Resorts as our primary development partner: they've been doing this for 30 years, and they know all the angles. Marc Roberts, a former sports agent and author of *Roberts Rules! Success Secrets from America's Most Trusted Sports Agent,* now backs SunVest, and he's taken Charles and me under his wing, introduced us to major players. When you meet people of all ages, it makes you realize you can do exactly what they have done. I always leave those events with ideas. Extraordinary achievements become ordinary daily business. It elevates your perspective. You go from thinking small to thinking huge. Changing my perspective has changed my life and made me wealthy. When I got into real estate I had a net worth of about $3,000. Now I own eight properties and part of a business and have a net worth of about $2 million. Not bad for just three years, and my net worth is steadily increasing as my property holdings appreciate.

Myth 6: Risk leads to financial ruin.
Truth: Wealth requires risk.

First of all, many risks have nothing to do with money, so this myth has no legs to begin with. But even in those risks where money is involved, taking them hardly has to lead to bankruptcy. In fact, quite the opposite is true. The most important lesson of this entire book can be summed up in the following Rule of Risk:

KENDRA'S RULE OF RISK 3

Taking a calculated risk is often the best way to create wealth for yourself.

As I'll describe in more detail later, after two issues of *Capture Life* had come out, Charles asked me to leave it behind and join him in the real estate business. I could have said no thanks. What would have happened? In all likelihood, I would have continued to toil long hours doing the jobs of three people, maybe pulling down a decent salary, and perhaps, in the future, being able to sell the magazine and finally cash in. But that's a lot of "maybes" to bank on. Sure, I would have enjoyed running something I had built and working in a business that I found stimulating. But I would have missed out on a huge financial opportunity.

By taking the risk, diving into a business I knew nothing about, getting my real estate license in 2003, working with RE/MAX to learn everything I could about the basics of buying and selling property, I was able to do more than build a successful company. I also earned enough and became savvy enough to do my own real estate investing, to the point where today I own enough property to give me a net worth around $2 million. Not bad for twenty-seven years old. But if I hadn't taken the risk, that financial opportunity would never have come my way.

Of course, some risks carry with them the potential for financial losses. That's part of risk: the greater the potential reward, the greater the risk of loss. That's why safe investments like U.S. Treasury bonds might pay 4 percent while junk bonds pay 15 percent; the risk is higher. But the only way a risk can bring you financial ruin is if you're foolish. If you invest every cent you have in a golf course resort scheme on environmentally sensitive swampland and the project goes belly up, you'll lose it all. But why were you so heavily invested in such a dicey scheme in the first place? Sound judgment protects you from financial losses that are too hard to take. That's not to say you won't suffer them. Robert Allen, the bestselling author of *Nothing Down* and other investing books, tells the story of how he lost everything in the space of a few months in 1986 when his multimillion-dollar seminar business went bust and his family's mountain home in Colorado was utterly destroyed by an avalanche (which happened about seven minutes before his wife would have arrived home). But that disastrous year led Allen back into his business with a renewed sense of mission and he's now bigger than ever, with new bestsellers and a series of hugely popular seminars.

Risk always suggests the possibility of loss. If it didn't, it would be called certainty. But as with so many things in life, it all depends on your perspective. With the right planning, judgment, and attitude, your odds of realizing great wealth through risk taking far exceed your odds of losing your shirt.

EXAMPLE: Some recent retirees I know are proof of the concept that without risk, you gain nothing. Back in 1975, when they were scraping by financially, they moved from their small town in southern California to a place where their children could get a better education. Scraping together every cent, they managed to buy a house for $45,000. They lived frugally and resisted the temptation to tap their growing equity, and when their children were grown and married and retirement time came in 2005, they were able to sell the house they could barely afford at $45,000 for $520,000—a profit of 1,155 percent. They walked away with enough to pay cash for a new home in a golf course community and pad their retirement nest egg—but it never would have happened had they played it safe as a young married couple and stayed in the house they could easily afford. Risk not only did not ruin them, it gave their children a high-quality education and made their prosperous retirement possible!

Myth 7: Risk is for the young.
Truth: Risk knows no age ceiling.

This is part of ageism that still infects our society, the idea that seniors should just keep quiet and grow old gracefully. I can't think of anything more absurd. Ever hear of John Goddard? When he was fifteen years old, he wrote down a list of 127 things he wanted to do in his lifetime, from trekking to the source of the Nile to retracing the route of Marco Polo. Today, he's eighty-two, he's reached the 127 goals on his "life list," and he's just made a new list of *five hundred* goals. Goddard is risk personified. When he dies (no doubt going over a waterfall while wrestling an anaconda) he should be made the patron saint of risk.

The people who believe risk is only for the young are the ones who reflexively associate risk with bungee jumping, crazy adrenaline-filled day trading, and starting Internet companies on a business plan and a prayer. In other words, they buy into the media portrait of risk taking as glamorous. The truth is different. Most risk takers are simply working hard every day trying to move toward a vision of a better life, a brighter future. You don't have to be twenty-five and single to be a successful risk taker. In fact, in many ways I think the older you are, the more risks you should be taking.

There are two reasons for this. First, as you get older, it's natural to want to slow down, to get into a comfortable rut and to stop taking risks. The minute you do so, however, you stop growing. You become a hothouse flower, able to survive only in a narrow range of conditions. You become one of those retirees who buy into the concept of golf and canasta as fulfilling ways to spend the last twenty-five years of life. You move into a retirement community with all people your own age. You bury that business idea you once had because you're too old for such things. You quit dreaming. And you wait to die.

Instead, I think older Americans should be on the lookout for risks—starting home-based businesses, traveling to new places, getting involved in the arts or politics, stepping out of long years of comfortable, familiar behavior into things that are, yes, a bit scary. But what a thrill to try choral singing and find out you're a natural baritone! Or to open an antique store and find yourself spending your days making money at something you love! Or what about moving out of the retirement community and into a busy urban downtown, surrounded by people of all ages, where you can walk to cafes, theater, and shopping? Sure, city streets might be unnerving for some people, but they are also exhilarating. As we age, we owe it to ourselves to consciously explore ways to continue risking, growing, and challenging ourselves.

The other reason I believe older people should take more risks is so obvious it's funny: they have more experience. I've been in real estate for just a few years, but I've learned by listening to people who've been in the business for thirty years and more. Do you think I'd do a deal with those people? In a second! Age and wisdom frequently go together: when you've lived sixty or seventy years you have learned how to read people, gained the ability to distinguish between reality and overblown promises, and built a network of contacts and friends from all walks of life, people whom you trust.

Older people have hard-earned judgment, perspective, and experience that younger people can't come close to matching. Those qualities can be tremendous assets in a business deal, an investment, or an entrepreneurial project. In fact, I think younger risk takers and older risk takers should ideally work together, one lending the energy and fire of youth and the other bringing to the table the discretion and wisdom of age. That would be the perfect team to turn risks into wonderful opportunities.

If you're older and you've spent a lifetime avoiding risk, it's wise not to start out with risks that are too much for you to handle. But there's no reason to avoid them. Truth be told, there's every reason to pursue them vigorously. Most aging experts agree that seniors who try new things and challenge themselves are more likely to stay vital in body and mind much longer than older people who are sedentary. See, risk is good for you.

EXAMPLE: I have some clients who are around sixty years old who had all their money in stocks. But when the market dipped after September 11, they lost hundreds of thousands and swore they would never go back into the market. So, working with me, they bought their first two investment properties at one time in July 2003. One cost $186,990, the other cost $182,990, and they put down only 10 percent so they didn't tie up all their cash. It was a surprisingly bold move for people who were supposed to be enjoying a risk-free retirement. Well, eight or nine months later, they sold the property that cost $183,000 for about $240,000, a 31 percent profit in less than a year. They still own the other property, and it's worth over $300,000. They are actively buying other investments. As a matter of fact, they just bought into a preconstruction project in Loreto Bay, Mexico. Age has not been a barrier for these people at all. I'd say their wisdom and discretion have been assets. Once they got a taste of investing and knew they could do it, they never looked back. I know people half their ages who can't boast as much.

Myth 8: Risks are always obvious.
Truth: Some risks will only be seen by the educated.

A risk worth taking won't always be staring you in the face. Sometimes, risks that can change your life are nondramatic events that barely register in your mind. If you don't recognize them, you might miss them. But if you can recognize them, you might find yourself with a rare advantage over the competition.

I think most people expect worthwhile risks to come in big, flashy packages: a once-in-a-lifetime investment opportunity, for instance. But more often than not, the idea of the bigger-than-life risk is just another Hollywood concoction. Most of the time, the risks you'll come across will be subtle, quiet chances to revector the course of your life: meeting someone who wants to talk about starting a new business with you, reading an audition notice for a local summer stock theater, passing runners in training for their first marathon. Each of these is an opportunity to stop, ask questions, make a phone call, say "yes" to a question, and start moving in a new direction. The question is, will you do it?

How do you start recognizing these quiet, under-the-radar risks? It takes developing your sense of what represents a risk, what is truly outside your comfort zone, and why. To see all the small risks that come your way, you've got to know yourself, know what makes you comfortable and what scares the daylights out of you. When you encounter a person, an audition notice, a business opportunity, or a sporting event, you've got to be able to ask yourself these questions:

1. Is this situation outside my comfort zone?

2. If it is, why?

3. Is it something I want to explore?

4. If so, what do I need to do?

Start asking yourself those questions constantly, whenever your mind runs across a situation or opportunity that's unfamiliar. Slowly, you'll train yourself to see the risks that others ignore because they're too busy looking for the bright lights and loud music.

EXAMPLE: Early in his career Charles was just doing finance, and he went to a new development to look into buying a unit as a personal investment. He skipped work to buy a house and waited in line all day for his opportunity to write a contract, sitting there with his hard-earned money, which wasn't a lot. He and everybody else in line were treated like dogs. And the people came out and said, "Don't worry, we're going to start a list, we'll see you tomorrow morning." He was furious about losing another day of work, but he really wanted to buy. So he went back the next day and not only was there no list, there was no one in the sales office at all. He still bought a unit, but not the one he wanted. Now, here's the difference between Charles and other people. Most buyers would have gotten angry, bought their unit, and sworn never to do business with that developer again. Charles saw an opportunity. He said, "There's got to be a system, organized and fair, that works better." He decided he would start a company that would give investors a system that brought us all in working together, where buyers could get educated and take advantage of economies of scale to buy at deep discounts that would give them instant equity. And that's how MyHouseRE.com was born, because Charles saw a worthwhile risk where others saw only poor customer service.

Myth 9: You have to be first in line for your risk to pay off.
Truth: If you're in the right place at the right time, it doesn't matter.

It doesn't hurt to be the first person to market with a new product or the first investor team to buy into a new condo community. In fact, having what's called "first mover advantage" can be a huge advantage in turning risk into reward. However, it's more important to handle your risk right than to be first. If I have to choose, I'll take the smart, well-managed team that started second over the first movers who don't know what they're doing.

Take computer operating systems as an example. Apple Computer was the first company to popularize and fully develop the graphical user interface, or GUI, the landscape of clickable icons you now use to control your PC desktop instead of typing in lines of obscure code like you did when computers took up entire rooms. However, it was Microsoft, using what Apple had done, that spread the idea of the GUI around the computing world by licensing its Windows operating system to other computer manufacturers to preinstall on their systems. Today, Windows, considered by most computer experts to be an inferior product, holds a hammerlock on the operating system market, while Apple's OS runs on a pathetic 2 percent of computers. It doesn't help to be first if you can't take advantage of the opportunity.

There are instances in which time is a factor in leveraging a risk and turning it into reward. I have been involved in real estate deals where I received a call and had to make a decision that day whether or not to invest. In such circumstances, all you can do is fall back on your better judgment. I usually go for it, and so far I've been fortunate enough to have such investments pay off. There are advantages to being first: you can lock up the market before anyone else is even aware you're in; you can get patents or copyrights to prevent anyone else from taking your route to profit; and, most of all, you can catch everyone else unprepared. There's nothing like getting into a market first to get great deals, before interest increases and drives up the price.

However, if the need to be first leads to recklessness and a lack of planning, it can also lead to disaster. You cut corners, you don't ask tough questions of vendors or lenders, you pay too much because you don't feel like you have the time to negotiate. That's when mistakes happen. If it comes down to a choice between acting first and going in blind or acting second and going in prepared for all eventualities, I'm inclined to go in later. You've got to judge based on the situation and the potential reward, but the higher the level of uncertainty, the more likely you are to benefit from slowing down and letting someone else blaze the trail for you.

That's one of the biggest advantages of taking more time to prepare: you let somebody else make the big blunders, discover the swampland under the construction site, the pending fraud charges against the would-be partner. I'd much rather let someone else stumble in going 100 miles an hour and reveal the potential pitfalls of a deal than waste time and money finding them myself.

Bottom line, there are advantages to being first and to being deliberate, but for our discussion, the key point is, you don't have to be the first horse out of the gate to win the race. It doesn't matter if you're ahead at the halfway point. It matters who crosses the finish line first.

EXAMPLE: In late 2005 a woman came to me wanting to invest. There was a close-out special at a condo project, Hamptons at Metro West in Orlando, that was almost complete. Usually, these properties are snapped up and gone, so normally I wouldn't have been able to help the woman. But one of the late buyers couldn't perform on contract, and the developer was motivated to get out of the project, so they put it back on the market for $26,000 under market value. Even sweeter was the fact that the developer was also running a special in which it paid the buyer's first twelve months' worth of Homeowner's Association fees, which in this community was $240 a month. My buyer jumped at the opportunity and bought her place for $226,990. She minimized her carrying costs, got $26,000 in equity at closing, and saved nearly $3,000 in fees the first year. The moral of the story is that you have to figure out what motivates people. Get inside their heads. At the end of a project, developers are motivated to sell and move on, and often they will add incentives and sell below market value to get out. Being first isn't important; being smart is.

Myth 10: You'll get to it someday.
Truth: If you don't do it when the chance appears, you won't do it.

This is the myth that breaks my heart, because I hear people say it all the time. They have a dream—to open a French bakery, quit their job to start their art career, invest in the stock market—and when I ask them about it, they say, "I'll get to it someday." I want to grab them and shout, "No, you won't! You'll keep talking about it until you're old and gray and too feeble to chase your dream! Do it now!" That's how I feel. I think it's a tragedy when someone has a dream that's within reach and fails to go for it when going for it would have been so easy.

If your attitude toward the risks that can transform your life is "I'll get to it someday," trust me, you will never do it. Because either you don't believe it's possible or you don't have the confidence that you can make it happen. Breaking out of a rut and stepping out of your comfort zone take energy, planning, and goal setting. It's not easy. Unless you take specific action to begin tackling the risk that you've been dreaming about, you will not do it.

For example, if you've always wanted to run a marathon, you know you can't just lace up your new athletic shoes and run twenty-six miles. You've got to train. You've got to start months in advance, running greater and greater distances to build your endurance and refine your technique to avoid injury. Only then can you run the marathon course and hope to finish at all. It's the same for any risk, whether it's starting your own business or buying your first preconstruction condominium. You've got to prepare, make plans, make decisions, and take positive, consistent action. If you keep telling yourself, "I'll get to it," that consistent action is impossible. There comes a time when you must simply act.

In her book *Unstoppable Women,* author and speaker Cynthia Kersey proposes that her readers embark on a thirty-day plan to change one thing in their lives. She holds that anyone can take one action, one day at a time, to achieve a worthwhile result. Kersey's theory is that if you can stay on target for thirty days and lose your ten pounds or write your business plan, you can apply that same approach to other aspects of your life. I love this idea, because it gets you into motion. Instead of talking about your risk or trying to jump into it with both feet before you're ready, you can take a step at a time, a day at a time. It's not glamorous, and it's not climbing mountains or ballooning across the world, but it is progress. You're moving farther from your comfortable rut every day. And that can only make your life better.

EXAMPLE: I had a client in late 2005 who had the opportunity to get one of only two units remaining at an exciting new Las Vegas community, South Gate Condominiums. He knew it was a good risk, but something stopped him and scared him at the last minute and he couldn't pull the trigger on the deal. He had the chance to get one of the best units I had available at the entry pricing of $254,490 and missed out. Those units will do nothing but appreciate hugely for the next five years, at least. Sometimes, you have to make the leap or miss the train.

DEVELOP YOUR OWN BELIEF SYSTEM

I've spent a chapter debunking these myths about risk because I feel it's vital for fledging risk takers to ignore the popular ideas about risk and reward and focus on developing their own belief systems about themselves and what they're capable of. Your belief system is the foundation of your risk taking: it will define how you respond to risks, whether you can see them coming or they take you by surprise. Like I said, I respond to risks the way I do because it's become my nature, and part of that nature is my belief system about myself.

What is my belief system? I'll share a few of its tenets with you:

— I'm capable of handling any situation that comes my way.

— I'm unafraid of making mistakes.

— I'm willing to jump into situations about which I know nothing and learn as I go.

— I know I will always rise to the top and land on my feet in any circumstances.

It's taken me a few years to develop that belief system, but I live by it today. It pulls together all the things I know to be true about myself into a succinct way of thinking, allowing me to reinforce my belief in my ability to cope with virtually any risk. It's important, as you venture into new areas of risk in your own life, to develop a belief system that reflects who you are, what you can do, and what you believe you are capable of.

Why does this matter? Because you are going to confront doubts. You are going to fail. You are going to run into people who will try to discourage you either through their own cluelessness or out of a desire to eliminate the competition. When you do, a firm belief in your own abilities and desires can help you get through those rough patches. For instance, people sometimes have doubts about working with me because of my age. When I first got into the business, I was twenty-four and I looked like I was eighteen. People were very skeptical about taking real estate advice from me. But because I believed so much in the product that I was investing in and endorsing—and believed in myself—they forgot their initial doubts. When I give speeches, I speak to people twice my age, and in the beginning there's a lot of skepticism and doubt, but people realize that I've had the experiences to justify my successes. I have several wealthy clients who have been in this business a long time and are in their sixties and they are now some of my best clients. They recognized some of themselves in me, because they, too, had a strong belief in themselves.

Take some time to ask yourself what you believe about yourself. Be positive. Look within yourself to find the strengths you carry around with you daily but maybe don't have the chance to express: your creativity, your physical fitness, your compassion, your ability to communicate with all kinds of people, your gift for team building and making everyone on the team feel important. Those are all important, useful qualities, and you can find ways to make them assets in your risk taking. But first, acknowledge that they exist. Develop a set of belief statements about yourself and repeat them to yourself at the beginning of every day, like a meditation mantra. You'll begin to transform your consciousness, and when you do that, you'll start to become the kind of person who can face any business or financial risk and come out on top.

3.
RISK AND REWARD

Risk! Risk anything! Care no more for the opinion of others, for those voices. Do the hardest thing on earth for you. Act for yourself. Face the truth.

KATHERINE MANSFIELD
THE JOURNAL OF KATHERINE MANSFIELD (1927)

Reward and risk. The two are bound together, which is something that purveyors of old folk wisdom seem to know better than the rest of us. Why else do you hear sayings like, "If you don't go, you won't know" and "Worrying about choking shouldn't stop you from eating" from grandparents or codgers standing around small-town general stores? They know that sticking to what makes you comfortable is a sure way to spend your life going nowhere. My professional life is about real estate, so that's where I've seen the relationship between risk and reward firsthand, but the principles that I talk about here can apply to virtually any part of business or life, because no matter where you look, risk and reward are inextricably linked.

Everything you do in life must be weighed according to reward and risk. Consider: you're planning a vacation. Should you drive or fly? Driving offers the reward of not waiting in airport lines and being able to stop along the way, but the risk of the tedium and fatigue of driving, traffic, and bad drivers, not to mention the cost of gasoline. Flying rewards you by delivering you to your destination in hours instead of days, but you run the risk of endless airport lines, rental car problems at the other end, even higher costs, and, of course, the tiny risk of a crash. Which reward outweighs the risk? That's what you'll choose to do.

The seventeenth-century mathematician Blaise Pascal developed a formula now known as Pascal's Wager, which he used to gauge whether a belief or risk was worth accepting. Pascal applied his wager to the question of whether it was worth it to believe in God (he decided it was, because the reward for being right—getting into heaven—far outweighed the risk of being wrong), but we'll apply it here to the idea of risk in general. The wager works like this: measure the benefits of a risk and the chance of those benefits coming to pass. Then measure the cost of the risk and the likelihood of those costs coming to pass. If the potential benefit is greater and more likely to occur than the potential cost, the risk is worth taking.

For example, let's say you are looking at starting an independent bookstore right around the corner from the local Barnes & Noble, figuring that the educated people in your city will opt for a quirky, intelligent, but more costly approach to literature than the discounted, big-box retail direction. If you ran that risk through the Pascal formula, you would see that the potential benefits include business success and an elevated standing in the community, but because the odds are inherently stacked against any small business succeeding, you would have to conclude that the chance of those benefits coming to pass is low. The cost of the risk is high—investment capital, large amounts of inventory, long hours, potential financial ruin if the store fails—and the powerful competition nearby makes the chance of the cost coming due for you pretty high. On paper, this is an unwise risk.

Of course, Pascal's Wager is a reductive way to approach something as personal as risk. There are factors that can't be boiled down to formulas:

passion, teamwork, duty to family, and so on. If starting an independent bookstore has always been your dream and you feel that you have the fire in the belly and the ideas to make it a success, you should do it. Maybe just not around the corner from a Barnes & Noble. The fact that you "went for it" is one of those intangible rewards for risk taking that are rarely mentioned but make it a lot easier to hold your head high at the end of the day. Don't discount emotional reasons for taking risks. But since no risk should be taken on pure emotion, the Pascal formula is useful because it helps cut through the haze of emotion and show you some hard facts about your risk before you jump.

THE RISK/REWARD OF THE EVERYDAY

I'm going to talk mostly about real estate in this chapter because it's what I know, but that doesn't mean I'm ignoring the fact that risk and reward are not inherent only in the high-stakes world of buying and selling property but in every aspect of daily life. You face risk/reward propositions from the time you wake up in the morning to the time to go to bed.

Take an enterprise that couldn't be more different from the world of real estate: launching a career as an artist or writer. Such a thing often involves leaving behind familiar surroundings and moving to New York, Los Angeles, or Paris, where you may have no support system or friends. You may not have to scrape together as much startup capital, but the risk/reward equation couldn't be clearer. On one hand, you have the potential benefit of living your dream, being independent and making a living from what you love, perhaps even acquiring elevated social status as part of the intellectual elite. On the other hand, most artists would starve if they had to survive on the income generated by their art. You face also the risk of loneliness, poverty, failure, and being forced to retreat back to your hometown with your tail between your legs, your dream dashed. It's not a scenario for the faint of heart.

Or how about another high-risk career: politics. These days, many of the politicians we see on the national stage are wealthy businessmen and businesswomen or attorneys who have made the decision to give up their private lives, spend millions of their own money, and work for years to reach high elected office—and for what? Public scrutiny, attacks from the other side, the frustrations of the partisan system. Politics is a meat grinder; it's no accident that presidents seem to age twenty years during eight years in office. The rewards are substantial: power, prestige, a chance to serve the public, perhaps global recognition and a lasting historical legacy. But the risks—scorn, scandal, subjecting family to the spotlight of the media, and so on—can be withering. For most, the price is too high.

The risk/reward dichotomy even extends into one of the most fundamental parts of human experience: raising a child. Imagine that you're a young couple and you're trying to decide whether or not to have a baby. There's no decision more fraught with consequences, and you find yourself weighing the risks and rewards. On one hand, money will become tight. You'll have hardly any private time for years. Maybe there's a history of some genetic illness in your family. And, of course, what if you turn out not to know how to be good parents? Couples face this decision every minute of every day.

Then again, you will have the joy and wonder of a child in your house, and the fun of watching him or her grow and change. New friendships will form with people who have young kids of their own. And there's always the possibility of grandchildren and someone to carry on your legacy after you're gone. Millions of people every year ignore the potential risks and decide to have children. It would be a poorer world if they did not.

Even my relationship with my coauthor, Charles Andrews, has risk. He and I have both a business and a romantic relationship. History has shown that to be risky; I once worked with someone with whom I was personally involved, and it was a disaster. Charles and I work beautifully together because we share some qualities and in other ways we are very different. It is rewarding personally and professionally, but it doesn't mean it's not a risk. Any time we trust another human being, we take a risk. Risk and reward are everywhere we look.

RISK AND REAL ESTATE

There's an old saying that real estate is the best investment because "they aren't building any more land." Well, aside from major landfill projects in places like Dubai, that's true, but it's only part of the story. I think real estate is also the best investment because it's the only instrument of wealth building that's always proved to increase in value over the long term. You'll see dips in the market here and there, sure, but if you bought a house thirty years ago for $20,000 in even the least-active real estate market in the country, it's virtually guaranteed to be worth at least $100,000 today. That's a nice return on investment by any standards.

Real estate is my business, my career, and my major hobby. I'm president of MyHouseRE.com, where Charles and I work to help investors build their own wealth by buying into condo conversion projects and pre-construction projects from South Florida to Orlando to Las Vegas, and soon in Arizona. And if that's not enough, I regularly buy rental properties in and around South Florida. I love buying properties, love the feeling of closing a great deal, love getting the rent checks every month, love taking good care of my tenants, and love knowing that I'm building wealth and security for the long term no matter what else happens in my life. Real estate is my hobby; it's just a lot more expensive than stamp collecting and doesn't make you sweat as much as mountain biking. Well, usually not.

I adore what I do, and one of the reasons is the elements of risk and excitement. Sure, there's a tremendous rush in closing a great deal, whether it's for my clients or for myself, but part of the thrill of the business also lies in the fact that it's filled with risk. There's risk in buying property: there might be structural problems, the market might take a dip (leaving me underwater on my loan), tenants could damage the place, bad weather (hurricanes in Florida, mudslides in California, for example) could leave me with an empty lot and a bunch of firewood. Stuff happens.

The ironic thing is, I've been lucky enough to avoid having any risky situations crash into total failures. I haven't been in the business very long, so I don't have juicy failure stories to share. Maybe, since I don't know one successful person who hasn't had at least one major failure, that means my crash and burn is still to come. So far, I've been fortunate enough to avoid major disasters. But I've certainly watched other people's ships go down due to bad planning, too many uncertainties, or just simple bad luck. And I've learned that the truly successful ones don't treat their monumental failures as endpoints, but as speed bumps. They learn and get back on the road, turning their hard lessons into future success.

NOLINEGROCERY.COM AND OTHER DISASTERS

Charles is a person like that. More than anyone else I know, he's had to overcome a lifetime of obstacles and failures to reach the success he's enjoying today with MyHouse. His father died when he was young and he had to get a job picking up trash on a farm to earn enough money to buy school clothes for himself and his sister. And yet he came from that background, which would have made many people bitter and angry, with two abiding qualities: the desire to help others and the fire of entrepreneurship.

That fire in the belly led to Charles's two great business failures. The first was an entertainment company he started while he was in college called Chuck's College Entertainment. "I was looking for a great way to pay expenses in college," he says. "We'd go into clubs and ask the owners how much they were pulling in each night. Then we'd offer to lease the place one night a week for six months, pay the owner more than they had been making, and bring in our own staff and rename the club for the one night. We'd transform the clubs and turn them into the hottest spots in town. The first night, even though there wasn't a person in the place, we hired a bouncer to keep people from going in and a guy to pretend to be a fire code enforcer saying he would shut us down if we let one more person in. The next night, the place would be packed, because everyone thought it was the one place everyone was dying to get into. It was incredible, but we just couldn't make enough to keep it going."

It's true to his indomitable spirit that Charles jumped right into more ventures, which set the stage for his biggest train wreck, a Web-based grocery delivery company called NoLineGrocery.com. Now, if you know anything about the history of the Internet and the dotcom boom, you know that grocery companies like Webvan.com have led a precarious existence. NoLine was no different. It was an idea whose time had not yet come, and it was in trouble from the outset. "Groceries is a high-volume, low-ticket, tiny-margin business," Charles says, "and we didn't own our own grocery store, so we had challenges even warehousing the groceries. Food rotted in trucks, and everything that could go bad did go bad in that venture."

That Charles bounced back to achieve tremendous success in real estate proves not only his resilience but his character as well; he had the wisdom not to burn bridges, fully aware that today's failed partnership can become tomorrow's successful one. "I paid back every dollar to every investor, $130,000 in all, even though I didn't have to," he says. "Their investment agreement stipulated that they were risking their money, so I could have said, 'Oh well, that's the way it goes!' and walked away. But there's what's right and what's legal, and they aren't always the same thing."

Charles understands—and has helped me to understand—that you must take risks and often rack up multiple failures in order to finally have great success and build the lifestyle you want.

RISK IS THE FATHER OF REWARD

It's one of the fundamental principles behind all kinds of investing: there is no reward without risk. In fact, that's an excellent axiom to follow in life: to reap great rewards, you must take great risks. The scale of your risk will determine the level of your reward. I think we can call that one of Kendra's Rules of Risk:

KENDRA'S RULE OF RISK 4

Risk is the father of reward.

Without risk, there would be no reward. Barring miracles, good things don't just fall out of the sky in your life, do they? If you want to build a multimillion-dollar retirement nest egg that will let you move to Maui at fifty, then you've got to accept greater risk in your financial portfolio than somebody looking to retire at seventy and live modestly. You've got to buy stock in more volatile companies, time the market, and maybe even buy high-rate junk bonds that offer a big potential payoff but zero security. The greater your risk, the greater your reward. The flip side to that is, of course, that you've also got a greater chance of disaster. You accept that chance in order to have a shot at the sweet payoff. That's a decision you make anytime you confront what I call a "risk/reward situation."

That risk/reward dynamic is why I love real estate. Because property is such a basic human need (you don't *need* to own Microsoft stock, but you do need a place to live), it's usually the least volatile investment in any market. The nature of real estate reduces the risk of loss and failure while its basic appeal to human beings makes it a wonderfully profitable long-term buy.

CHANGE IS THE BAROMETER OF RISK

Just as risk is the father of reward, change is the barometer of risk. Real estate is one of the safest investments around because it is *change resistant.* The more conditions can change in and around your investment, the greater your risk of your investment's going down the tubes. Volatility is really about how vulnerable your investment is to forces that alter it from what it was when you invested your money. As Warren Buffett and his fellow "value investors" have demonstrated, all risk/reward calculations must take time into account. They invest in things that have underlying long-term value, so if volatility impairs profit in the short term, they can still profit in the long term.

Here's an example. Let's say you're an investor back in the heady days of the Internet boom, around 1998. Dotcom companies are popping up everywhere, going public and piling up huge market caps that have nothing to do with reality. You're looking to make your fortune fast, so you invest $100,000 in the stocks of a few of these new companies, based on the idea (the hope) that the bubble won't burst. You're buying major volatility in return for the chance of a high payoff in two or three years, when you hope you can sell your stock for a million dollars and retire early.

Why is this a dangerous investment and a foolish risk? Because it's too subject to change. There are dozens of ways in which the forces that make your investment potentially valuable could change violently in a very short time. A new technology could appear and make their business models obsolete. A CEO or two could embezzle millions. Politicians could decide to levy a sales tax against e-commerce or somehow regulate it. Investment banks could withdraw needed capital. Or the stock market could go belly-up, which is exactly what happened. Goodbye, $100,000. And those are just a few of the changes that could devastate your investment.

I'm not saying don't buy stock in companies. I'm saying that by buying stock in unproven companies that have never shown a profit, you leave yourself open to radical change that destroys value. Because you measure your risk not just by your vulnerability to change, but by the *likelihood* of that change's occurring. Buying stock in Dell, General Electric, or Wal-Mart buys you the security and track record of those companies, companies that weather change extremely well and aren't likely to vanish overnight.

Real estate is the world's best investment because it's so change resistant. If I buy a four-unit Palm Beach rental property that's in good shape and in a decent neighborhood, what change factors could my investment be subject to? The market could go downhill, but in a coastal area, that's not likely, and if it did, I would just hold onto my property until the market rebounded. There could be a hurricane, which happens here. But I'm insured, and the chance of my property's being severely damaged is small. My neighborhood could become infested with gangs and drugs, but that's also unlikely, since it's actually becoming more affluent. Zoning laws could change, allowing undesirable development in the area, but I can influence zoning laws by talking with local politicians, so they're not completely outside my control. And that's about it. The property isn't going to move farther from the beach, people aren't going to stop needing homes, and since

I bought a fixed-rate mortgage, my interest rate isn't going to rise. The factors that make my investment valuable are unlikely to change much, if at all. My risk is very low. My barometer reads clear weather ahead.

There's a very basic wisdom to this, one that Buffett, Fidelity stock whiz Peter Lynch, and other market titans have followed: you rarely go wrong when you have an eye on people's essential needs. People will always need health care, so while a particular health company stock might crash, a health care index fund is always going to trend upward, because folks will always get sick, have babies, and need root canals. The same is true for what I do: people will always need homes. Paying attention to people's needs is a great way to reduce your risk.

CAPTURE LIFE

I started my real estate career in early 2003. Before that, I was the founder and coeditor of a local lifestyle magazine. I had graduated from the University of Florida with a degree in linguistics, and I couldn't get a job. So, in what was probably my first embrace of risk as an adult, I created my own job. I and three other budding entrepreneurs decided to start a magazine. I had been waiting tables, bartending, and doing odd jobs, and I had saved about $10,000. I realized I was going to have to live off that money while we started the magazine. I literally had to sit down and decide whether I was going to take that risk. I had worked hard to save that money, and I was living paycheck to paycheck. With the magazine, I would be spending more than I was making. But I felt the reward—starting a magazine, being editor in chief—was worth the risk. Our business plan was simple: create the ultimate guide to the South Florida luxury lifestyle—fashion, real estate, dining, travel, celebrity. We figured upscale advertisers would beat a path to our door.

The result was a glossy quarterly called *Capture Life*. I'm a believer in the idea of *carpe diem*, or "seize the day," and I wanted the magazine to reflect that belief, that you have to take big handfuls of life when you have the chance, because the chance might not come around again. The magazine was not just about fashion and food, but about adventure and water sports and even ecology. I had a chance to work with Philippe Cousteau, which was amazing. He's close to my age, and here he is traveling the world, completely inspired, spreading the message of protecting the oceans. He was living his dream and so was I.

I didn't know anything about starting a magazine when I jumped into *Capture Life* in late 2001. I went to the library and checked out books about the magazine industry, basically took the Magazines for Dummies course. But there's no teacher like experience. As I said earlier, we had a partner's father as a financial backer, and he ended up capitalizing us for a total of $300,000 (ironically, he was a physical education teacher in Coral Springs, Florida, who had made his money in real estate), but I wasn't making any money. It didn't matter to me; I was learning. At some point I said to myself the same thing I would advise anyone who wants to change his or her life to say: "I'm not afraid of making mistakes. I'm not afraid of jumping into something that I know nothing about."

So I learned to work with writers and photographers, negotiate with advertisers, handle contracts, find and negotiate with printers, and so on. It was an incredible experience. I never took a business class, and everything I learned I learned through trial and error. We lost $66,000 on our first issue, less on our second. When I left in December 2002 we had put out only two issues, but I obviously helped lay the groundwork for something pretty good; *Capture Life* is still around; sells for $4.95 an issue at bookstores, airports, luxury hotels, and restaurants; has a circulation of about 42,000; and has won several design awards from the Florida Magazine Association. I'm proud to have helped get it started.

MYHOUSERE.COM

A combination of relatively low risk and consistent long-term value has made me thrilled to be a part of MyHouseRE.com. Our mission is simple: to provide affordable ways for investors of all incomes to begin building a foundation for wealth through investments in real estate. Charles and I locate two types of real estate projects (only in Florida and Las Vegas at present): condo conversions (where rental apartment complexes are being converted into condominiums) and preconstruction condo projects, where we're in touch with the developers before construction even starts.

MyHouseRE.com is a matchmaker, linking those projects with people who want to buy one or more units as investments. We're really about managing risk, not selling property. We focus a great deal on educating our clients and helping them make smart, risk-moderate investments that are right for their goals. As a licensed Realtor, I broker the final deals. It's a hugely successful model; we get buyers from as far away as the Midwest and California. Buyers are able to get a below-market price by getting in early, especially on preconstruction projects. The developers are delighted because they begin to recoup some of their costs before they even break ground. Everybody wins, and that's when business is sweet. There are also two other aspects to the business: United Mutual Lending, our mortgage lending arm, and MyHouse Productions, which handles public relations and marketing.

Charles started what was then called MyHouse in 2000 after seeing hopeful investors passed over by developers because they were stuck on interest lists, waiting for the chance to buy properties. Interest lists are databases developers create of people with an interest in buying their units, but typically the only benefit to being on an interest list is that you learn that units are for sale a few days before the general public. You're guaranteed nothing. If there are 2,000 people on a list and only 200 units, you still only have a 10 percent chance of buying. These people were playing the lottery, unable to buy other properties while they waited.

Charles thought it was unfair, so he launched MyHouse to connect investors with developers equally eager to reduce their own risk by preselling a large percentage of their project. Today, we reach would-be buyers through broadcast and print advertising, media coverage, and our radio program (more on that in a minute), and we've built a high-performance, high-velocity business that will—if we reach our goal—help 1,000 clients buy investment properties in 2006.

In 2002, my magazine invited Charles and his team to a big event because they had advertised in our first two issues. I guess Charles saw something in me, because he chased me for six months trying to convince me to join his company. At first I was reluctant, because I had worked so unbelievably hard to build *Capture Life* and now it was off and running. But as time went on and Charles kept calling, I started to get curious about the real estate world. And that's where my natural proclivity for risk kicked in. If I left the magazine, I'd be risking giving up what I had created to go into something I knew little about, but I had already done that in starting *Capture Life*. The potential reward for that risk was considerable: the challenge of a fast-changing, exciting business and potential wealth beyond what I would ever earn as a magazine publisher.

I was making less than $20,000 a year at the magazine, and I knew real estate offered the potential to make ten times that or more. Eventually, the allure of the money and challenge became too great, and I left to join RE/MAX, earn my real estate license, and work with MyHouse. I've never regretted the decision.

RADIO DAZE

Apart from the risk we deal with every day at MyHouse in working with investors and developers, we took a major risk in growing the company and increasing its visibility, including something few real estate companies have ever done: we started our own radio program in 2003. Charles and I knew that we were offering people something of tremendous value—an opportunity to get ahead of the market and create wealth through real estate investment. But how to set ourselves apart from the pack of other real estate companies? How to establish our credibility? Charles hit on the solution: a radio program dedicated to the preconstruction and condo conversion investment market.

So the MyHouse radio show was born. Every Sunday on Clear Channel station WBZT in West Palm Beach, Charles and I go on the air for an hour to talk about the Florida real estate market with our listeners and promote our own projects. It's been a winner, but the venture wasn't without risks. Even though I was a state high school debating champ in Virginia, the thought of going on the air with 100,000 people listening made me nervous; Charles was just as anxious. We had elected to pay for airtime so we could advertise our own projects instead of having advertisers, but that meant we stood to lose money. Neither of us had any radio experience. We were risking our image as a company and as individuals. What if we bombed?

We didn't. We knew the premise of the show—real estate talk in a region where real estate is one of the primary topics of conversation—was a winner. There are two competing shows in the market, but the difference is that they're 90 percent sales and we're 90 percent education. By the time you get to the sales pitch with us, our listeners are sold. Intelligent people can recognize a deal without being told it's a deal. Now we sell properties from the show all the time; I've gotten calls from buyers during the broadcast. I'd say we make about a 400 percent return on our airtime investment. That's another risk that has paid off handsomely.

A FORMULA FOR TURNING RISK INTO WEALTH

MyHouseRE.com has become an enormously successful, profitable enterprise. Perhaps the most important aspect of that success is our carefully calculated formula for managing risk and creating profit. The formula is simplicity itself:

1. Invest our clients in properties that are five years old or newer. The reason is that newer buildings are in better shape and more likely to have the modern amenities that tenants want, such as waterfront location, golf course, tennis court, indoor basketball court, fitness center, computer room, library, and wireless Internet access.

2. Invest them in properties that have a price point that 96 to 98 percent of people can afford. That's what we call a "recession-proof"

price point. With a recession-proof price point, no matter what the market does, you'll always be able to either rent your property, sell at a profit, or carry the mortgage until the market improves. It's a price point that almost anyone can absorb. At the time this book was written, that price point was about $300,000 in South Florida, Las Vegas, and Phoenix. But as the market changes, that price point shifts.

3. Get them to diversify as soon as possible. Stockbrokers are always talking about diversification, and it's a great strategy. I'd rather see my clients own ten $200,000 properties than one $2 million property. Why? Versatility and liquidity. If the market takes a downturn, they won't be able to get $2 million for that mansion. Plus, not all markets go bad at once. If you're in Orlando, West Palm Beach, and Las Vegas, what are the odds that all three will experience a downturn at the same time? Practically zero.

Making money in real estate is really common sense. Be the lowest-priced house in the highest-priced neighborhood. Have the right project in the right place. We went into Port St. Lucie, a town where the single-family home market has been red hot, and selected a condo community surrounded by single-family homes. When we got our investors into it, we found that because the demand for condos in the city far outweighed the supply, they were getting great rents and building tremendous equity.

Every truly successful risk taker has a formula. Warren Buffett, the country's second-richest man after Bill Gates, found his formula for choosing stocks in the writings of Benjamin Graham, whose book, *The Intelligent Investor*, has been in print since 1949. Buffett read the book when he was an undergraduate at the University of Nebraska, studied with Graham at Columbia University, and then worked with him in the professional world. Along the way the "Oracle of Omaha" developed his system for choosing and mitigating risks: knowing not just a company's business plan and profit/loss statements, but the skills and character of the people running it. A quote on the Berkshire Hathaway website illustrates this view nicely: "If you don't know jewelry, know the jeweler."

For MyHouseRE.com, the key is that we *never* deviate from our formula. Most people in real estate will get pumped about a project and start thinking with their heart instead of their head; that's when they make stupid mistakes. MyHouse always sticks to the formula, and it enables us to introduce thousands of people to the wealth-building potential of real estate with minimal risk.

MANAGING RISK

As I said before, MyHouseRE.com is really not in the business of locating and brokering investment property. We're in the business of managing risk for people who might otherwise be afraid of it because of the unknowns involved. We eliminate 99 percent of the unknowns, making it possible for us to provide affordable investment for people who might otherwise waste their time in low-return investments.

Based on our experience with investors and our own experience buying and selling properties, Charles and I have come up with a list of six guidelines for successfully managing risk, not just in real estate, but in virtually any business or endeavor. Depending on the area of risk, you may find there are other factors that help you reduce your risk, such as education or personal relationships, but these basic rules will form a strong foundation for any potential risk/reward situation, from investing to starting a business:

1. Have a formula of your own

Your formula will vary depending on the business you're in, but you should come up with a standard formula and then never deviate from it. For instance, if you're buying condos in the red-hot San Diego market (one of the most out-of-this-world markets around right now), you might have to develop a formula not based on recession-proof pricing, but on speed, because properties sell so quickly there. Or let's say you're in Texas and you're "buying and flipping," acquiring rundown homes, rehabbing them, and re-selling them quickly. Your formula might revolve around only buying homes of a certain condition or never offering more than a set percentage of a property's market value. Have a specific plan and adhere to it.

Every formula will be different. The key is to find yours, keep it simple and clear (I suggest no more than four components), and then stick to it 99 percent of the time. The other 1 percent, have fun. My formula is basically the same one I apply for my clients: it's all about education. I'm in the business of prequalifying them, advising them on the best price point, determining their short- and long-term goals, advising them on flipping (selling a property within weeks of closing for fast cash) and selling, all based on personality and their financial picture. I walk them through the deal, act as their realtor, educate them on financing, risks, tenant issues, and beyond. I do the same for myself in my formula:

a. **Locate multiple opportunities.** By staying in touch with developers, networking with investors at my REIC, or Real Estate Investment Club (a great resource; learn more at www.reiclub.com), and watching the print and online media, I can learn about properties before 90 percent of potential buyers do.

b. **Educate myself.** I become an information junkie. I want to know population growth figures for the area, how the employment base is doing, any redevelopment plans that are on the drawing board, proposed commercial developments that might be happening in a three- to five-mile radius, availability of tenants, and sale prices of comparable properties in the area. Based on that information, I determine my recession-proof price point.

c. **Get my ducks in a row so I can create a win-win.** Just as I do for my clients, I assess my risk tolerance at the time; it changes as the market changes. If the property fits my risk tolerance, then I get everything I need in order: cash, financing, insurance, paperwork. My goal here is to make things easy for the seller, Realtor, or developer; I want to create a win-win so if there are competing buyers, they'll go with me. I make sure I can close in the shortest time possible, that my money is ready to go, and that I've built a transaction that, from my end, will go as smooth as silk. That makes sellers and developers love me.

d. **Act fast and mitigate.** Once everything is set, I trust my experience, data, and knowledge and I move. I don't wait for doubt to set in. I make my offer and see what happens. Sometimes I get the property. Sometimes I don't. But I'm always a player. And because I mitigate no matter what (remember the Ates?), I'm always networking, making a new contact, or learning about a new property or neighborhood.

2. Understand your product

This seems so basic, but I'm always shocked at how many people get into real estate without really understanding how the type of real estate they're in works. Single-family homes, from how they're built to how they're marketed to how they're valued, are different from attached homes like condos and townhouses. Rentals are different from buy-and-flip properties. Single-unit rentals are different from multi-units. Heaven knows residential is different from commercial, and commercial that's designed for retail is nothing like commercial that's designed for a resort, manufacturing, or offices.

I don't like the stock market, because I don't have a deep understanding of it. But I understand condos. I understand rental properties. I understand how developers work and what they're looking for when they agree to do a preconstruction sale. I know more than just the construction details behind converting apartments to condominiums. I get the mindset of the developers, I know the amount of capital that's involved, I know the geographic areas, and I know the past and present state of the markets in those areas. I understand the field of real estate I'm in. You must do the same. Whether your business is nightclubs, a sports league, or a political action committee, get to know your playing field like you know your own neighborhood—the people, the market, the money, the technology, the legal issues. All of it. Then you won't be surprised as often, and you'll be comfortable enough to take risks.

When I went to work with Charles I didn't know much about real estate except that I wanted to. I knew that the financial backer for *Capture Life* had made his money in real estate and that most of our advertisers were developers, so I knew this was a field I *wanted* to learn about. So I opened my ears, got my license, talked to experienced RE/MAX agents, went to every REIC meeting, and asked questions and talked to everybody. I didn't make a dime in my first six months, but I soaked up information, and when I thought I was ready, I went out and bought my first investment property.

Here's the thing: you won't ever think you're ready for your first deal. You just have to do it. Nothing teaches like experience, making a few mistakes, and realizing that yes, you can do this.

KENDRA'S RULE OF RISK 5

If you wait until you feel 100 percent ready to move, you will never take the first steps.

3. Have a great Power Team

Your Power Team consists of all the people whose services you need to make your business run. In real estate, that means a lawyer, lenders, title company, contractors if you're into rehabilitating homes, messengers, maybe a design firm and a printer if you print brochures and other materials, and so on. If you're in the clothing design business, that could mean modeling agencies, photographers, fabric suppliers, and public relations consultants. Everybody on your Power Team should be the best in their business, people who know their work and whom you can trust to deliver what they promise on time. That's not easy to find; there are a lot of flakes out there. But once you find a great Power Team, they'll help you make a lot of money. Of course, you've got to take care of them in return. Treat them right. Give them bonuses. Refer business back to them. Create win-wins. That's always a smart strategy.

The best way to find Power Team members is to talk to the people at your REIC. Ask them who they rely on; personal references are better than any advertising. You can also talk to developers about individual contractors and businesses they use. After all, with millions at stake, they're not going to trust exterior detail carpentry to someone without a long track record of success. Do not place classified ads, and don't waste your time calling people in the phone book. You don't want to teach someone how to do business with integrity and respect for your time. You want someone who already does both.

4. Learn when to walk away

I'm an aggressive risk taker in my own real estate investing, and I'm quite bold and action oriented when it comes to my business, but that doesn't mean I'm reckless or foolish. I may trust my gut, but that doesn't mean I turn off my brain. In my mind, I have a list of qualities that make a risk unacceptable for me. Whenever I look at a risk/reward situation, I run down that list in my head and see if the situation has too many of those qualities. My attitude is, if I'm on the fence, I walk away. I don't worry about it and I don't look back. There are always more opportunities coming along, so why force myself into a situation that may be less than ideal?

KENDRA'S UNACCEPTABLE RISK FACTORS

Too many elements beyond my control
People with questionable integrity
A price above my recession-proof price point
Location in an economically doubtful area
Property age or structural problems

It's critical that you develop your own mental list, one that applies to the field where you're taking risks. For me, the unacceptable risk factors revolve around one thing: excessive uncertainty. The more uncertainty involved in a risk, the less comfortable I am in taking it. Of course, uncertainty is inherent to risk. If you don't have any, it's not a risk; you're firmly in your comfort zone and going nowhere. But uncertainty comes in levels and types: uncertainty about money, about people, about government, about weather, about the market, about the economy, and so on. Some uncertainty can be planned for: if you're looking at investing in a rental property and you're uncertain about the local rental market, you can buy and hold the property or wait and see what the market does. But some uncertainty is beyond your control: too much competition in the same price range, concerns about the integrity of your partners, the uncontrollable vagaries of hurricane season. If I were offered a chance to buy into a golf course resort that was going to start construction anywhere on the Gulf Coast in September, the height of hurricane season, I would pass. That's an unacceptable level of uncertainty.

What is your unacceptable level of uncertainty when it comes to risk? It's crucial that you discover that, memorize it, and live by it. Know when to walk away from a risk that rises above that level. That kind of self-discipline, not to allow yourself to let your starry-eyed dreams overrule your sense, separates smart risk takers from everyone else.

KENDRA'S RULE OF RISK 6

There is a level of uncertainty where a risk becomes unacceptable to all but the foolhardy.

My level of unacceptable risk is quite high; that's my nature. But I'll walk away from a deal if I think it's trying to defy the market (too many of the same properties in one area, for example), if the numbers don't add up, or if I have concerns about the integrity of too many of the key people. Your threshold will be different. Learn what it is and don't deviate from it.

5. Learn about people

This might be the most important of all. Every risk will involve people in some way—partners in a business venture, your spouse in a decision to have kids, your team in a mountain climbing trek, and so on. How well you choose the people in whom you place your trust will often determine whether your risk pays off or is a failure.

In starting *Capture Life* magazine, I had to decide whether I trusted my college friends enough to live on ramen noodles for months and spend every dime I had to support myself while the magazine was starting. I chose to trust them because I knew their characters, knew they were talented and hardworking and as passionate about the project as I was. They took the same leap of faith in me, and the result speaks for itself: a magazine that's still going strong. One of the founders, designer Jesse Kain, is still involved, but now he's editorial/creative director.

To take successful risks, you must hone your people skills to as keen an edge as your business skills. Talk to everyone you can, not just about what they know, but *who* they know. As your circle of contacts in your field of risk expands, you will begin to hear the same stories about people: he's a hard worker, she bluffs when she doesn't know, he tends to pad the numbers, and on and on. Develop a healthy level of skepticism about anyone promising you what appears to be a dream deal; always ask to see the numbers or the product. People who can back up what they say won't hesitate to do so; those who can't will find excuses to avoid doing it. They're the ones to walk away from.

As with your unacceptable risk level, the kinds of people to work with and avoid will vary according to each person. But for me, there are certain qualities that paint a big red "NO" on a person's forehead:

— He/she is known to falsify financial information or other critical data.

— He/she finds excuses not to share financial information with me.

— He/she has a reputation for dishonesty.

— He/she pretends to know more than he/she does.

— He/she is careless or reckless.

— He/she has a problem with full disclosure.

Just as with unacceptable risk, develop your own list of qualities and live by it. When you encounter people with those qualities, don't hesitate to say "No thanks" and walk away. There will always be other deals, other adventures.

At the same time, know what you want from the people you work with. One of the things I look for is someone who can recognize the intrinsic value in something like a coastal property or a golf course property. I like to work with people who demonstrate vision, who can look at a piece of property or a project and see not what it is, but what it can be. Those are the people who change the world, who can perceive something of value in a real estate project, a small business, or any other pursuit and find a way to make it happen. While you're figuring out the qualities you want to avoid in people, take some time to catalog those you want on your team.

6. Talk to (and listen to) everyone

I already mentioned this in regard to learning about people, but there's a better reason I've learned to pick the brains of everyone I meet who's more experienced than I am: I want to learn from the failures of others so I can avoid failure myself. I'm stubborn, but I realized that maybe I should listen and learn from other people, learn about their mistakes so I could avoid my own catastrophes. I make it a point, whenever I can, to listen to people who are older and wiser than I am, people who have been in the real estate business longer than I have, which is almost everyone. And I've discovered that everyone has a story. They all have life lessons and wisdom, even if they don't realize they are sharing them with you. So I started talking with people and I heard their horror stories about buying insurance from fraudulent insurance companies, about working with people who cooked the books and made up financial numbers to cover losses or to make poor performance look better. I asked questions, then I shut up and absorbed. I still do it today. And at the end of the day, I make a few notes to remind myself of the things I heard.

What my habit of listening has done is helped me compile a list of things not to do: don't trust certain insurance companies and so on. But eventually, a list of things not to do also becomes a list of things *to* do, best practices and wise choices, good people it would be a pleasure to work with on any venture, and so on. Become a conversation junkie and learn from the people who have made the mistakes you'd like to avoid.

EXAMPLE: I go to meetings of my local Real Estate Investors Club, talk to everyone I can, and learn all the approaches to making money in this business. There are many different types of real estate investing: rehabilitating houses, short sales (when the outstanding debt on a home is greater than its resale value), foreclosures, preforeclosures, lease options, condo conversion—and even within those sectors, everyone has their own style. I ask how-to questions and listen to how people go about accomplishing their deals. For instance, there's a guy named Mike Perl, who wrote a great book called *Checks Don't Lie,* who last year probably bought and flipped close to 200 preforeclosure homes worth more than $12 million. Mike knows all the tricks, and when I listen to people like that even if I'm not in that business at the moment, I'm more prepared if I run into an opportunity in that area in the future. For example, right now, everyone wants to get into preforeclosures, so for every property there are several hundred investors vying for it. But I listen and learn from Mike, because while everyone else is calling and sending letters, you know what he's doing? Mike will go up and put a FedEx package on the doorstep of a house in preforeclosure. Do people open FedEx boxes? Of course they do, every single time. So while these people are being bombarded by calls and junk mail, Mike is the one getting in the door. That's the kind of thing you can learn only by listening to the veterans.

BUT WHAT'S THE MOTHER OF REWARD?

If risk is the father of reward, there's got to be a mother, right?

KENDRA'S RULE OF RISK 7

In real estate, the mother of reward is timing.

You can have the best deal in the world, but if your timing is off, it will turn out to be a dud for everyone involved. Or you can have a weak deal, but if the timing's fortunate, it can still be a bonanza. Again, the same is true no matter what your area of risk is. Timing is everything.

In my business, timing is critical because everything that determines the value of real estate occurs cyclically. The health of the local economy, local real estate prices, interest rates, the popularity of a neighborhood, the condition of that neighborhood and the city or town around it, the trendiness of architectural styles—they all run in cycles that can last for years or even decades. When interest rates are down, the housing market booms. When crime is up in an area, prices drop with demand. These days there's constant talk of the real estate "bubble," the bull market we've had in residential properties since 2000, fueled by the unbelievably low cost of borrowing. Well, I don't believe in bubbles, not in a healthy market. Will prices go back down after they've been high? Of course. That's part of the cycle. Will you be hurt if prices drop? That depends on your timing. Did you buy at the peak? Or are you poised to buy during the dip and make a killing?

Anyone who tells you he can time

"The refusal to rest content, the willingness to risk excess on behalf of one's obsessions, is what distinguishes artists from entertainers, and what makes some artists adventurers on behalf of us all."

John Updike, author, on J.D. Salinger, *Christian Science Monitor*, 1965 the real estate market—or any market—with 100 percent accuracy is lying to you. It's not possible. However, making big money in real estate depends to some degree on keying your action or inaction to the timing of the market. So how do you know to act at the right time? Mostly, you learn the forces that drive your specific market, then you keep your eyes and ears open. Every real estate market is driven by a unique set of forces. In South Florida, the most important forces are retirees, the weather, and developers. In other markets, the major forces might be environmental regulation, traffic, crime, lack of buildable land, toxic soil, or a dozen other factors. Interest rates and the sale prices of local properties shape the development of every market. It's up to you to learn the forces that drive your market, then watch them like a hawk, because they'll tell you where your market is going. That knowledge will enable you to time the market to some degree, giving you a valuable edge in buying or selling.

What are the key timing-related forces that drive the risk that you're involved in? If you're writing the business plan for your retail business, is the market for what you'll be selling in your community growing or shrinking? If you're investing in the stock market, are you buying shares of a strong company on the rise based on good fundamentals, or are you buying into a bubble that's sure to burst? If you're daring the bubble, do you know when to sell before it's too late? You *must* know the timing of the market you're entering. That's important because of the next piece of advice I'm going to give you.

BE READY FOR THE MARKET, DON'T FIGHT IT

KENDRA'S RULE OF RISK 8

You can't fight a market.

There was a developer in late 2005 who was planning to build a condominium tower in Miami at a cost that he thought was going to be about $83 million. But this market is very volatile; fuel costs are sky-high, and with Hurricanes Katrina and Wilma—as well as demand in China, believe it or not—the costs of cement, steel, copper, and gypsum (used in drywall) are expected to rise. So the tower project that was supposed to come in at $83 million looks like it's going to cost more than $150 million, because the developer didn't understand the market, tried to defy market conditions, and failed to lock in his costs. Now, it looks like he'll end up being sued, because he has taken deposits and can't build the project, and possibly forced into bankruptcy. The lesson: know your market and walk away if things aren't right.

History is littered with wrecked investors who, if they'd paid attention to prices in their area, they would have seen them already beginning to drop. Or investors who've roared into a neighborhood and decided to buy the six worst properties on the block, fix them up, and bring the neighborhood back to life. That's a great goal, but if the market is still held down by the perception that the area is unsafe, there's not a thing that investor can do to change that perception. Markets are about emotion as much as money, and emotions are unpredictable and uncontrollable.

Markets are like the wind. Timing, a success formula, and smart risk taking are like sails. They can capture the wind and harness it to take you where you want to go, but they can't alter it or influence it. The same is true in any business, and in any aspect of life. How and when any milieu—from an economy to a social trend—progresses is beyond anyone's control. All you can do is hone your skills and be ready to pounce when opportunity appears.

Markets are bigger than you, me, or anybody. They are forces of nature. Even if a billionaire comes into a city and spends $200 million buying 200 residential properties, he's not going to alter the fundamental movement of the market. Sure, he'll drive up prices somewhat, but unless the market is very small, he alone won't shift a down market to an up market. Federal and state governments can move markets with their enormous spending power and ability to change interest rates, but even that's rare. Markets are made of millions of moving parts—people, properties, financial institutions, laws, and beyond. They determine themselves.

So trying to fight a market is to be like King Canute, the English monarch who gave orders to the ocean in vain. You can't fight a market. What you can do is use your knowledge and experience to understand it, watch the forces that drive it, and know when the timing is right for you. Fortune favors the prepared. Then when the market shifts in your favor, you can ride the wave as far as it will carry you—or you can get out of it if conditions shift against you. Understand your market, prepare for it, but don't try to fight it. Bend with the wind, then when it shifts in your favor, ride it for all it's worth.

LEARN THE RULES, THEN BREAK THEM

In our talk about real estate, I've thrown a lot of rules and principles your way. That's because this is my business—my life, really—and it's complex. It's a great way to make a ton of money, but it's also an easy way to lose it. So it's essential to know the basic forces and guiding wisdom that underlie the profession; if you decide that your life-changing risks will come in real estate, the rules will be your flotation device as you're learning to swim.

But in the end, of course, the real fun lies in mastering the rules so you can defy them when the time and opportunity are right. It's like learning the fundamentals in baseball. If you want to play shortstop, you've got to learn the boring, repetitive mechanics of fielding ground balls. When you have the fundamentals down cold, you can snare a slow-moving grounder with your bare hand and throw on the run. You can throw out the textbook fielding techniques you've mastered because you know playing it by the book won't get the job done this time.

In real estate and any other business, you absolutely must learn and live by the fundamental rules about timing, having a Power Team and a formula, understanding what sells and doesn't sell in your market, and so on. Those rules comprise your foundation, and 98 percent of the time your success will depend on sticking to those rules. But that other 2 percent— once you've got the fundamentals down, that's where the fun comes.

Here's an example: Let's say your business is focused exclusively on condominiums. You've been in the business for about ten years, and you have a great network of contacts and a deep understanding of your market. Then a historic, beautiful Victorian home in a quiet neighborhood comes up for sale for $400,000. Normally, you wouldn't even look at it because it's outside your core business. Plus, it would require $50,000 worth of updated plumbing and electrical and Internet wiring as well. Furthermore, single-family sales in your market are cold. But this time, you take a look, you negotiate, and you buy the place. Why? Because you recall a local developer's telling you a few months earlier that he would love to open his own bed-and-breakfast as part of his retirement, and the Victorian would be perfect. You get the financing, buy the house for $380,000, then immediately flip it to the delighted developer for $450,000 in fifteen days, walking away with a $70,000 profit and leaving him to take care of the rehabilitation costs.

You violated your own rules about staying within your market and not buying high in a down market, and you made money. You were able to do it because your fundamentals were strong: you have a personal network that already dropped the buyer in your lap, and you knew the location of the house was ideal for a B&B. You were able to act on gut instinct backed by knowledge. You broke the rules and got away with it.

Learning the rules so you can make your own is one of the most enjoyable aspects of smart risk taking. I certainly don't defy my rules for buying investment properties very often; I have a formula for success and I stick with it because there's no good reason to deviate. But it's comforting to know that my skills, experience, and judgment make me capable of jumping into an irresistible deal without being blind and reckless. I can enjoy the ride and be confident that I can handle whatever comes along. That's when real estate really becomes a thrill.

RISK CHANGES THE WORLD

From time to time, I need to reassure investors that the risk they're taking with MyHouseRE.com is a wise one. When that happens, I'll ask them to look around them. Look at the landscape of Palm Beach. Look at any big city. Look at the incredible project in Dubai on the Persian Gulf, where the government there is using landfill to create a huge palm tree–shaped peninsula running for miles into the ocean. On this man-made land, they'll build luxury hotels and houses selling for millions. It's one of the most marvelous and ambitious things I think the hand of man has ever done, and a perfect illustration of the principle I share with my clients: *dramatic change is risk made visible.*

People are surprised when I tell them you can see risk. But you can. It's not ephemeral. Every time you see a skyscraper, a new bridge connecting Denmark to Sweden, a trendsetting novel in literature, or an incredible advance in medicine, you're seeing risk in its physical form. Every dramatic change to the landscape and culture, from buildings and harbors to new laws and award-winning films, is a manifestation of someone—an individual, a company, or a government—taking a risk to reach a future reward. When you think about risk that way, it becomes apparent that taking risks is not just a luxury for skydivers and empire builders. It's how civilization advances.

You can find examples of the transforming power of risk in every facet of human civilization. For example, the Human Genome Project, started in 1990, spent $2.7 billion and employed hundreds of scientists at twenty sequencing centers in China, France, Germany, Great Britain, Japan, and the United States in a high-risk venture: to catalog the complete sequence of the *three billion* base pairs that comprise human DNA. At the outset of the project, its goals were thought by many to be impossible, but they were achieved in thirteen years, and the genetic knowledge that has been produced is already transforming medicine.

Or how about the risk involved in Sun Records' signing of an obscure singer out of Memphis named Elvis Presley in 1955? Until that time, only black singers were recording rhythm and blues music; "white music" was defined by performers like Pat Boone or Ricky Nelson. But Elvis rose to stardom as a white boy singing the music of the Mississippi Delta, and in doing so opened the floodgates for what would become known as "rock and roll," transforming the musical landscape of the world.

Until 1947, an unwritten agreement between baseball club owners kept African-American players out of the major and minor leagues. That is, until Brooklyn Dodgers president Branch Rickey chose Jackie Robinson to break the game's color barrier. It was a risky move that forced Robinson to endure terrible racism on and off the field from verbal attacks to death threats, and could have alienated white fans. But Robinson held on and played brilliantly. His courage inspired teammate Pee Wee Reese, a southerner, to not only refuse to sign a clubhouse petition calling for Robinson's removal from the team, but also to put his arm around Robinson on the field, effectively declaring to players and fans, "This is my teammate and friend." As more black players excelled in the majors, the calculated risk braved by these men led first to a greater societal awareness of racial issues such as the integration of the armed forces by President Truman, then to the work of pioneers like Martin Luther King Jr. and Rosa Parks, who helped launch the civil rights movement. Who would have thought that a brave, risky move on a baseball diamond could forever alter a society? It did. Risk changes the world.

You can see this same power that risk has when you look at any real estate project. Before a project is built, the land might be flat and featureless, empty lots or derelict commercial property. But after the project is built, you have a streetscape of attractive homes, maybe golf courses, paths, nature trails, and open space. The landscape is changed once again. And if you're an investor, you're an agent of that change.

Whether your risks come in real estate or other ventures, it's worthwhile to think of them in this light. Risk is a force, a power that leaves nothing unchanged. Whether that change is positive or negative is up to you.

4.

MARS, VENUS, AND RISK

Security is mostly a superstition. It does not exist in nature, nor do the children of men as a whole experience it. Avoiding danger is no safer in the long run than outright exposure. Life is either a daring adventure, or nothing.

HELEN KELLER, *THE OPEN DOOR* (1957)

Martha Stewart is an amazing woman. In the early 1970s she was a model, then a stockbroker. But in the late 1970s and 1980s, she began a catering business and started writing articles on topics like cooking, gardening, and entertaining for major magazines like *Family Circle*. More important, she had begun to develop her razor-sharp sense of brand development, and had started to morph into the doyenne of gracious living.

Next came a position as a spokeswoman for Kmart, her own magazine, *Martha Stewart Living*, and her first book on weddings. In short order she had landed a syndicated TV show, launched one licensed product line after another, and in 1999 founded Martha Stewart Omnimedia as a vehicle for her huge and growing brand. The company went public and she became a mega-millionaire as well as a cultural icon, parodied by everyone from Jay Leno to *Saturday Night Live*. Along with Oprah Winfrey, Martha was seen as the most valuable female personal brand in the country. Her risks—quitting her Wall Street career, launching a media venture (something I know plenty about), and taking her company public—created tremendous wealth for her and her shareholders.

Then in 2003 she was indicted on charges of insider trading in the stock ImClone Systems, a biotechnology company. Though the most serious charge, securities fraud, was thrown out, Martha Stewart was convicted in March 2004 of conspiracy, obstruction of justice, and two counts of making false statements. She famously received a sentence of five months in federal prison, five months' home confinement, and two years' probation.

Now, what does this have to do with women and risk? Plenty, when you look at how public opinion swung during and after her trial. In the face of the vast, multibillion-dollar frauds at corporations like Enron and WorldCom, Martha's transgression, though serious, was small potatoes. But the *schadenfreude*—the delight in someone else's misfortune—seen in the media and the public was astonishing. People reviled Enron's Ken Lay and WorldCom's Bernie Ebbers for what they did. Ebbers lost everything and received a twenty-five-year prison sentence. But though her transgression was minor in comparison, people seemed to hate Martha not because of what she did but because of who she is: the uppity "bitch" who had the temerity to live more beautifully and show more poise than them—and build an empire worth billions.

VICTIM TO HEROINE

If Martha Stewart had been a man, no matter how successful, she would not have received the venom she did from the American public. It's okay for a man to take audacious risks and build empires; it's something like unseemly when a woman does it. That's not to say she shouldn't have taken risks; Americans love to build up heroes, then tear them down in any case. And the public was responding to her well-crafted "Ms. Perfect" persona as much as her gender. But there's no denying that when it comes to risk and bold achievement, there are ways men and women are *supposed* to behave. When they don't, the reaction can be intense.

In this chapter, we're going to zoom in on your own gender-specific risk taking so you can become more aware of your own strengths and weaknesses and reap more and bigger rewards.

MEN AND WOMEN APPROACH RISK DIFFERENTLY

Andi Gray, a strategy consultant and president of Strategy Leaders, Inc., a Chappaqua, New York, business consulting firm, makes the point that as entrepreneurs, men and women approach risk from very different directions. She writes in the *Westchester County Business Journal,* "Successful men and women entrepreneurs are characterized by their high risk-taking profile—a core requirement for entrepreneurship—balanced with intelligent choices about which risks to take . . . Almost all entrepreneurs have significant capacity to challenge themselves, get out of their comfort zones and strive to take on skills and confront fears to move ahead. This is where the differences begin. Male entrepreneurs tend to be characterized by movement: an action-oriented style, focused on getting things done and moving on. Women tend to get hung up in the search for perfection . . . the 'dotting i's and crossing t's syndrome.' "

Gray's additional views on male

> **"Who wants a world in which the guarantee that we shall not die of starvation entails the risk of dying of boredom?"**
>
> **Raoul Vaneige, Belgian Situationist philosopher, *The Revolution of Everyday Life* (1967)**

and female entrepreneurs dovetail with my own. Female entrepreneurs tend to be nurturers who find themselves compelled to address needs outside the core areas of their business; trying to "fix" everything. Men, on the other hand, are more prone to delegating to subordinates and focusing on a single mission. The nurturing tendency often helps women develop empowering managerial styles, but can slow the pace of a company's competitive moves. On the other hand, male leaders often provoke action but are perceived as cold and uncaring.

And as Gray points out, women seek venture funding for their startup businesses far less often than men. I think this is due to two factors: bias against women in the male-dominated venture capital world, and women's desire to retain more control of their businesses. And that brings us full circle, back to the differences in risk attitudes. Control is a method for minimizing risk; the less your company's management is influenced by an outside agent, the lower your risk that an individual acting without your knowledge or approval could make a decision that would bring the business down. Men, however, tend not to have a problem with surrendering some measure of control of their business in return for capital. That suggests that men are more willing to accept the uncertainty of another party's having a dominant voice in the direction of their company. Two approaches, both effective. Is one better?

VENUS LOOKS, MARS LEAPS

A Korn Ferry International/Future Step research report from 2002 called "Vanishing Talent: Risk, Reward and Recognition" surveyed more than 350 British executives about their patterns of leaving safe corporate jobs for risky entrepreneurial ventures. Across the board, the survey found that women who strike out on their own were heavily in need of recognition and the opportunity to reinvent themselves. They loved calling the shots and controlling their business. No big surprise there. Some of the key findings taken directly from the survey:

— 99 percent of female entrepreneurs cited being able to fulfill their personal vision as extremely rewarding, while for men it was a combination of time for family, recognition for accomplishments, taking risks without repercussions, and not needing to fit in.

— 85 percent of men and 88 percent of women cited the "lack of a benefits package" as a less satisfying aspect of leaving corporate life to start their own business.

— Further top reasons both men and women entrepreneurs left corporate life were to take risks with new ideas and test personal limits, and to have more strategic input into decisions.

— Men stated money as the second most popular reason to change jobs, along with opportunities for strategic input, whereas women ranked it fifth, behind risk, recognition, and spending more time with family.

It appears that men are more inclined to approach risk as a competition with the tangible results as the rewards, while women more often seek intangibles as their rewards. To some extent, the stereotypes are true: women are usually less bullish than men, less inclined to rush into a situation with guns blazing. That's not to say that women are risk averse. I believe there's a greater desire for control among even women like myself who are daily risk takers.

When men take on a risk, they do so because they relish the challenge as much as because they've analyzed the facts and come to the conclusion that the rewards outweigh the risks. To be frank, men are more likely to be reckless, emotional risk takers. That's ironic, because women are supposed to be the emotional ones. However, when it comes to deciding whether to leap into a risk/reward situation, women are prone to more careful analysis of all the data. Women want to know how to evaluate the risk, how to control it, how to neuter it if possible. Women don't want surprises; men get off on them. Men might understand how to mitigate and minimize risks, but they're less likely to put that knowledge to use.

A Few Examples

— A man decides to launch a new company. He looks for the "big idea" and once he's convinced he's found it, he gathers a team of believers and heads straight for the venture capitalists looking for $2 million in financing. A woman in the same situation analyzes the market, her competition, financial projections, and more and solicits opinions from business contacts she trusts. It takes her much longer to make the jump, which could cost her first mover advantage.

— A man and woman partner to open a gourmet grocery store in a busy downtown area. As they divide the responsibilities, a pattern appears. The man takes on the preopening tasks that require schmoozing, deal-making, and networking: negotiating a lease, cutting deals with local newspapers for advertising, working with the banker to nail down a $250,000 business loan. The woman takes on the more detail-oriented, creative tasks: designing a logo, choosing and ordering inventory, writing advertisements, building a website. The business needs both to survive.

— A husband and wife each map out their ideal retirement portfolio. His is a bold, aggressive collection of securities from leading-edge companies in volatile industries, stocks that could rise like rockets or sink like stones. But if the market remains stable, they'll earn an average of 14 percent annually on their money, which will enable them to retire early. Her portfolio is more conservative, well-researched and balanced, the kind of proposal a professional financial planner would present. Her plan would produce steady results with a lower risk of major losses, a more reasonable 8 percent a year. The downside: they'd have to wait until age sixty-five to retire.

— A man and woman are buying a $600,000 Boston home together. This is where things change. Now, the woman is emotional and makes her decisions based more on how the house makes her feel than on the state of the market, what the neighborhood is like, or interest rates. Her husband, on the other hand, has turned into Mr. Analytical. This is because, in general, men are more focused on the tangible and the factual, on long-term value and growth. While women handle the day-to-day finances in 60 percent of American households (according to a study conducted by the Ohio State University Center for Human Resource Research in 2003), men are far more likely to handle investments like retirement accounts. The man will size up the risk of the property by checking out comparable properties for miles around, hire an engineer to inspect the slope geology of the lot, and shop around with a dozen lenders for the right package.

In every case, neither approach is wrong. This chapter isn't about right and wrong. It's about the fact that men and women do approach risk from very different perspectives. Don't agree with these examples? Ask yourself what you would do in each situation. If you've been in them, what did you do?

TESTING VERSUS TESTOSTERONE

I'm the first person to admit that this material is subjective and paints with a broad brush. Generalizing about men, women, and risk ignores the fact that there are plenty of men who handle risk more like women, and a fair share of ladies who respond like men when a risk pops up.

I'm actually more male in my approach to risk. I plan and prepare, but I also get a gut-level rush from closing a high-wire deal or buying a new property out from under two or three other sellers. I see risk taking as a competitive sport; that's very male. So I know firsthand that some men and women don't fit the mold I'm sculpting here. But most do, so the goal is to get you to examine your own approach to risk.

But up jumps the core question: Why? Why do men and women diverge so greatly in their methods of assessing and handling risk, a dynamic I like to call "testing versus testosterone"? I think the answer lies in our fundamental natures.

Women are childbearers. That makes them nurturers, more cautions in their actions because a woman's top priority is to safeguard the welfare of the family. So when risks appear, we approach them from the same cautious path. If it's too risky—if it might endanger the family—then women often back off.

Men were historically the hunters, the fighters, the warriors. Their lives, short as they often were, were packed with risk, death, and glory. Lacking the ability to give life as women can, men became creative in their own way, building empires, bridges, and corporations. Men are builders by nature.

However, in today's modern world, men's old roles aren't what they used to be. Although we still need warriors, architects, and visionary developers, there's little need for hunter-gatherers, and the great world-shaping projects that obsessed the likes of Andrew Carnegie and Leland Stanford are no more. All the while, women still have their primary role of creating life. So what's a man to do to satisfy that DNA-deep need for challenge, conflict, and victory? He starts companies, bungee jumps, and runs for Congress. He embraces the same emotions and thought processes— audacity, aggression, surprise, and blind courage—that served him well hunting lions on the veldt.

So today, you find a majority of women in business taking risks in a

> **"There is something about jumping a horse over a fence, something that makes you feel good. Perhaps it's the risk, the gamble. In any event it's a thing I need."**
>
> **William Faulkner, *National Observer*, 1964**

careful, considered way—perhaps a little slow on the trigger, but always with all the information at hand, and with a series of relationships set up to support them. And on the other end of the spectrum, you have business-men doing the same research but relying on it less, trusting their gut and looking at the risk/reward situation as an opportunity to give an idea life, to build something of consequence. The results? Very unalike. Women's mistakes will often be less serious, but their successes less dramatic, while men will tend to go into orbit or crater spectacularly.

Naturally, nothing is this simplistic. But it's impossible to deny. At the heart of the difference between men's risk taking and women's is that fun-damental fissure in how they view the world: as something to understand and preserve versus something to conquer. Testing versus testosterone.

WHAT MEN AND WOMEN LOOK FOR

So with all those opinions raining down, what are men and women look-ing for when they decide if a risk is worth taking? Based on the research

WHAT MEN WANT IN A WORTHWHILE RISK:	WHAT WOMEN WANT IN A WORTHWHILE RISK:
Competition	Compelling evidence
Adrenaline rush	The chance to analyze and weigh all options
To buck the odds	
Challenge	A surplus of information
Innovation	Wide-ranging relationships with people who will help
Intensity	
To be first	Recognition
Investment, even if it means surrendering control	Control, even if it means passing on investment
An experience that's exciting and educational, even if the risk fails	Emotional satisfaction
	Win-win situations
A band of brothers who go to battle together	A less intense timetable
	A good chance of success, because the pure thrill isn't that important

I've read and my own experience, the criteria are—no surprise—quite different.

When you're sizing up an opportunity that involves risk, whether it's in business or your personal life, you will probably find yourself fitting into these two patterns, more or less. Being aware of your own inclinations in approaching risk will help you approach it wisely and productively.

WHAT MEN AND WOMEN FEAR IN RISK

If you're gonna have one, you've got to have the other. Where there's a love of risk, there's fear of it, too. We all fear the unknown to a certain extent, and that's what makes risk, for many people, so impossible to resist. Because the only thing we enjoy as much as risk taking is confronting our fears in an effort to conquer them. Risk forces us to do that by speaking seductively at first, setting us up with conditions that we know about and can control. Then risk spills the real story: "A, B, and C could all happen and there's nothing you could do to stop it." By taking informed risks, we also become uncomfortably informed about all the things that could go very wrong. Ignorance is bliss, but ignorance won't do squat to launch your company or get you to the top of a mountain safely.

Just as it's critical to understand what's driving you to choose a risk, it's equally pivotal to know why you're pushing aside certain risks. So . . .

WHAT MEN FEAR IN RISK:	WHAT WOMEN FEAR IN RISK:
Boredom	Lack of control
Weakness	Alienation
Retreat	Conflict
Being a copycat	Envy
Dishonor	Poor preparation
Being second	Gender bias
Making poor judgment calls	Condescension
Betrayal	Failure

Make your own list—what's driven you away from risks in the past? What do you fear in a risk/reward situation? The more you understand your fear, the better your odds of conquering it—or of seeing that you were right to walk away each of those times.

MORE MARS OR VENUS?

As psychologists are fond of pointing out, we all have a male and a female side to our personalities. In each of us, the strength of each side varies. Some men are 99 percent male, others are 50-50. Some women are very masculine in their behavior. And, as you might have guessed, the same holds true in our risk tolerance.

How male and female are you in your ability to recognize and respond to a risk/reward situation? Take this brief test and find out:

MALE/FEMALE RISK QUALITIES

1. When an acquaintance approaches you with a "can't miss" business opportunity that requires a $250,000 investment, you:

    (a) Write him/her a check.

    (b) Ask plenty of questions and consider getting involved.

    (c) Ask for a prospectus and a meeting with the principals before you make a move.

2. You are offered a job at a fascinating startup company, but it will mean leaving your secure job. You:

    (a) Take the new job for the stimulation.

    (b) Tell your boss about the opportunity and ask her advice.

    (c) Decide your security and current relationships are too valuable to lose.

3. Just before buying a $300,000 condominium, you hear a rumor that the local real estate market is about to crash. You:

> (a) Soldier on, figuring rumors are for suckers.

> (b) Read everything you can get your hands on and make up your mind based on the data.

> (c) Invest elsewhere.

4. You get word that a developer that's desperate to sell the final $275,000 units in a condo community is giving $25,000 discounts to buyers who can close in fifteen days. You haven't been investing in real estate, but you know the community and the area are sure to appreciate. You:

> (a) Pull together a down payment and financing and do the deal.

> (b) Spend the weekend doing research, figuring the risk of losing out is worth a little due diligence.

> (c) Lose sleep over the money you might lose instead of anticipating the profit you'll make when you sell in a year for $350,000.

5. An employee under your supervision is causing problems. You handle it by:

> (a) Confronting him.

> (b) Talking to others to see if they also see the employee as a problem and why.

> (c) Engaging him in conversation to try and discover what might be wrong.

6. As you're preparing to launch your new company, you find that a rival is starting a similar company. You:

> (a) Speed up your schedule to beat them to market.

> (b) Rework your business plan or talk to them about partnering.

> (c) Trash your business plan and start over.

7. Your company has the chance to spend $1.5 million for a sixty-second Super Bowl TV ad. It will consume your entire year's marketing budget, but if it's successful, it could double your business. You:

    (a) Write the check and create the ad, all the time thinking, "Apple, 1984."

    (b) Watch every Super Bowl ad ever created, trying to make up your mind.

    (c) File the idea away and stick to advertising in the local paper.

8. You're self-employed and you get thirty days' notice that you're going to lose your biggest client, the source of 40 percent of your income. You:

    (a) Feel energized by the challenge of going out and finding new business.

    (b) Feel some panic but make a plan to pursue new business.

    (c) Feel great panic, but make a plan not only to pursue new business but drastically cut costs.

Scoring

Give yourself one point for every (a), two for every (b), and three for every (c).

    8–12 points: You're male dominant. You favor action, conflict, and the thrill of the chase in your risk situations.

    13–19 points: You're risk balanced. Your male and female sides complement each other, blending aggression with caution.

    20–24 points: You're female dominant. You favor caution, planning, and relationships over what you see as recklessness.

You may even fall somewhere in between these categories: a woman with strong female risk tolerance but with some strong male qualities. As I've said throughout this chapter, understanding why you take certain risks and reject others will help you take conscious control of those decisions, instead of being reactive.

THE PROBLEM WITH ASSERTIVE WOMEN

The problem is that some men and women can't handle them! I know, because I am what most men would consider an assertive, bullish woman. In the male parlance, I'm "ballsy." And I wouldn't change that about myself. But it does drive me crazy when I see the double standard that's out there, especially in the business world. It goes like this: if a man is no-nonsense and aggressive, he's a go-getter. If a woman behaves in exactly the same way, she's a castrating bitch. In my experience, it's a gender issue, not an age issue. I get the same reaction from men my age and from men over seventy. There are men who simply cannot process the idea of an assertive woman who is just as capable and successful as a man. It's not right, and I'm here to both set the record straight and encourage more women not to back down.

To me, the big issue lies in the difference between being seen as *assertive* versus being seen as *aggressive*. Being assertive means you stand up for yourself, insist on what you believe is right, and don't back down easily. If you're asked to take a risk, you demand information and don't budge until you get it. Being aggressive means you attack, instigate, and relish conflict. In a risk/reward situation, you're willing to make enemies to advance the cause.

Within reason, both are perceived as being positives in a businessman. But while it's okay for a woman to be assertive, it's less okay for her to be aggressive. It all has to do with perception. Women are perceived as being the nurturers, the communicators, the ones with the emotional intelligence. And those are great things, real benefits. But they're not all we are. Some women are also aggressive risk takers with just as much capacity as a man to dive into a new business venture for the adrenaline rush. That doesn't mean they're not feminine, and it doesn't mean they're not nurturing. It just means they know what they want and aren't going to fool around when it comes to getting it.

WE LOOK AT OTHERS BASED ON
OUR OWN COMFORT LEVEL

I believe that the bias against assertive and aggressive women, especially in male-dominated businesses, comes from risk-averse people. Those who would call me aggressive are probably risk-averse themselves. They've locked themselves into a certain status, and they label everyone else based on that status. Their disdain is a product of their discomfort with someone who's doing things in a way that they don't dare. It's a product of shame and embarrassment, folks. I'm afraid to be like that woman, so I'll tear her down instead!

Doesn't it make more sense to build up the risk takers, especially if they defy expectations for your own gender? If Martha Stewart, Oprah Winfrey, and Meg Whitman (CEO of eBay) are wildly successful, why are we so quick to tear them down? Is it because they're breaking society's rules about what success means for a woman? Or is it that they've gone places most men don't even dare to do? I think that's the real reason. I think it's those people who really have the problem.

GET A LITTLE PEANUT BUTTER IN YOUR CHOCOLATE

There was an old commercial for Reese's Peanut Butter Cups, where two guys, walking down the street while they're eating, bump into each other. "You got chocolate in my peanut butter!" one cries.

"No, you got peanut butter on my chocolate!" says the other.

Both: "Hey, they taste great together!" Ever see that one?

Just like that old Reese's ad, the male and female sides of risk taking taste great together. They're the yin and the yang of success—equal measures of action and compassion, relationship building, and empire building. In fact, the "Sex and the City" report, commissioned by financial services group Virgin Direct and directed by social anthropologist Kate Fox, codirector of the Oxford-based Social Issues Research Centre, offers concrete evidence that true success stems from a balance of the male and female halves. The study concluded that the combination of women's inherent financial caution and men's willingness to throw caution to the winds was the perfect psych profile of a successful investor.

The report states that "(women) don't like taking risks and are often happy to let the menfolk make the main decisions. Men, on the other hand, see financial risk as a part of life, something to be accepted, or even enjoyed. This willingness to take often irrational risks, such as day trading, can be put down to their evolutionary hard wiring."

Back to genetics again, the hunter-gatherer and the nurturing mother. But there's also a cultural side to it. Fox states that some women play their investments safe because financial products are intentionally marketed at men, who are in turn more gullible and willing to believe grandiose financial claims because they relish the element of risk.

From the study I quote Gordon Maw, marketing manager at Virgin Direct, who says, "It's abundantly clear that both men and women could learn from each other. Many women acknowledge and regret (that) their tendency to play safe is holding them back. If they adopted an element of calculated risk, their financial decisions could become significantly more lucrative. Equally, some men could benefit from being more rational about the risks they take."

Pop culture translation: you've got to have both peanut butter and chocolate if you want to have great taste and a winning candy recipe. This study shows what many of us already know instinctively: the male and female sides of risk taking don't have to be opposed. They can work together: discretion tempering impulsiveness, aggression turning planning into action. We need both sides of our risk personalities to be healthy and successful.

THE POWER OF DEFYING STEREOTYPES

I speak to women's groups, and my core message is pretty straightforward: *gender doesn't matter.* If you're a man or a woman, the only rule of the marketplace is get out there, work your tail off, and make good things happen.

Take *smart* risks, however you prepare for them. When I hear women talking about the glass ceiling and how they're conditioned to overprepare for risks, I'm tempted to say, "Just shut up and work." I'm a woman, and I don't overprepare myself or suffer from paralysis by analysis; I see risks, *quickly* analyze whether the opportunity will disappear if I take the time to investigate the people and properties involved, and if the opportunity is of short duration and the reward potential outweighs the risk, I jump at it. It's become a conditioned response for me.

Like it or not, it's mostly a man's world in business. Women are surrounded by guys in ties. Women's behavior with regard to risk is judged against the standard—men. That's the way it is, but that doesn't mean women have to be defined by the stereotypes of being timid and overly analyzing in taking risks. In fact, I've found that stereotype to be a strategic advantage.

How? Simple. I turn it on its head and defy it. I'm a very bold, take-no-prisoners businesswoman; that's my natural approach. But throughout my real estate career, I have run into men who assume that because I'm a woman, I will naturally be less decisive and less likely to make an aggressive move to capitalize on an investment opportunity than a man would. So I let them go ahead and assume that. And thinking that they don't have any competition, the men do what most people do: they get complacent. They waste time or act sloppily. Meanwhile, I'm eating their lunch. By the time they realize that I'm far more of a threat than they thought I was, I've bought a property out from under them or closed an exclusive deal to represent a condominium conversion company. For women, going against type can not only be satisfying and empowering, it can be a business edge.

The same is true for men who refuse to live by that "gung ho" stereotype and take the time to carefully investigate the risk/reward situations that come their way. With this approach, you may not find as many men who steal an opportunity out from someone else's nose, but you'll find plenty who avoided a disastrous investment that other guys jumped into, high on adrenaline. I've seen it before: an all-male group of investors or partners, pumped up on the thrill of the risk, pressures another guy to join in. It's half male bonding, half venture capital. And the new guy resists heavy pressure, questions about his manhood, and so on, to do his due diligence. He finds that the venture is built on shaky ground and finds the guts to resist the peer pressure, to say, "Pass." His would-be partners scoff and tell him he's missed the boat, then in six months lose their shirts. Again, defying stereotypes can pay off.

IT'S NOT A GENDER THING

In the end, taking risks should not be about gender, but about preparedness, confidence, and the willingness to get up one morning and proclaim, "I am not afraid to make mistakes." In fact, what I tell women when I speak to them is not to separate themselves from men according to how they approach risk. Just look inward to find the aspects of your risk-taking personality that are strengths, and make the most of them. You're not going to be perfect at every aspect of risk taking; nobody is. But you are going to be judged against men and how you perform in a man's world, so be the best you can be.

If you're a woman who is an obsessive planner, you should try to cultivate your gutsy, gung-ho side a little more. You should also look within yourself to discover if your planning is really masking fear. But at the same time, turn your natural risk style into a strength. If you're prone to planning and preparing, then become the most knowledgeable, educated, prepared, foresighted risk taker around. Be the woman thinking three steps ahead. You may miss out on some short-duration opportunities, but with the ones you do buy into, you'll be equipped for success.

And if you're a man who's prone to classic male risk behavior, jumping in with both feet before you even know if there's water in the pool, do the same. Yes, it's wise to cultivate your preparing and planning side, but while you're doing so, turn your aggressive, fast-acting side into a tactical weapon. Have your Power Team in place, with designated cell numbers that tell them instant action is called for. Be able to pull together in hours contracts or financing that takes the competition days. Strike fast and without fear. Jump at opportunities and learn as you go, like I did with the magazine. You will find yourself in over your head once in a while, but you'll also be counting your profit from some deals that slower parties missed.

It's wonderful to have a balance of impulse and planning. But if you can't, you can't. Make the most of what you have and who you are, and don't worry about what your chromosomes may say.

GET A "DIVE BUDDY"

In a few chapters I'm going to introduce you to the concept of "risk diving," my device for describing the act of taking bold risks that you mitigate with planning. I bring it up now in this context to make a point: having both a male and female side to your risk taking is wonderful, but if you don't have one side, get yourself a "dive buddy" who has the gender qualities that you lack.

In scuba diving, you always go underwater with a dive buddy. He or she is your partner, there to make sure you don't get into trouble and run out of air. In the world of risk and opportunity, your dive buddy goes risk diving with you to bring qualities to the situation that you cannot. If you're very male in your approach to risk, a female dive buddy brings rational thinking, planning, and a focus on relationships into each situation to balance your natural "leap before you look" tendencies. And if you're classically female, a male dive buddy modifies your intensive analysis with a touch of boldness and immediate action planning.

This really works. Why do you think Charles and I are so successful? There are many reasons, but one of them is that we complement each other. Each of us brings something to risk situations that the other does not. If you begin to see male and female risk-taking qualities not as separate but as equal parts of the whole, you can do amazing things.

5.

ENTREPRENEUR IS JUST "RISK" MISSPELLED

There is nothing more difficult to take in hand, more perilous to conduct, or more uncertain in its success, than to take the lead in the introduction of a new order of things.

NICCOLO MACHIAVELLI, *THE PRINCE*

Americans love entrepreneurs, so much so that we forget that starting a business—or more to the point, creating something new that we didn't even know we needed—is the ultimate high-wire act. But the view of entrepreneurs as wild business thrill seekers—skydivers who may or may not pack a parachute—is really not accurate. In fact, the word *entrepreneur* originates from the French word *entreprendre,* which means "to undertake." Nothing about risk or investment. But in our modern lexicon, the word has become synonymous with someone who goes out on a limb to launch a new business, usually in the face of either fierce competitive pressure or market indifference. Either way you slice it, being an entrepreneur makes you both an American hero and one of the most misunderstood creatures in the animal kingdom. But what does it mean to be an entrepreneur? Are they born or can you make yourself into one?

THE PONTIAC TASK

I'm a businesswoman, but like all people, I have a field where I feel most comfortable. As I've made clear, it's real estate. When I'm outside the bounds of the real estate business, I'm usually outside my comfort zone. But in 2004 when I was a candidate on the NBC reality show *The Apprentice,* dealing with each week's new business task, I was forced to confront my discomfort with what I didn't know about. For those of you who don't watch the show, two teams of candidates compete each week in a business-related task, the ultimate goal being for one person to be hired to work for Donald Trump.

That brings me to the Pontiac task, which was my defining moment on the show. The task was to create a new high-end marketing brochure for Pontiac's new Solstice sports coupe. I told my teammates that it would be an all-night task; coming from the magazine publishing world, I know that design work is very time-consuming and often takes many, many drafts; I knew this task would be the same. I had a very difficult decision to make. I took a huge risk by deciding to challenge my teammates instead of fighting them. I said, "If you want to go home, if I can't convince you to stay, you obviously don't want to win badly enough." Those who want to win don't quit. I ran a huge risk that my tactics would backfire. My teammates worked until about 3:00 A.M., but the majority of the design, the copy, and the creative decisions were done between 3:00 A.M. and the 8:00 A.M. deadline. I was all alone, and I brought the project home. I had no choice. The final result? I was the one Mr. Trump hired.

People forget about the home stretch. That's when things come together or fall apart. I wasn't going to tie my teammates to a chair; I had to challenge them and hope they responded. It was a calculated risk; I didn't plan on their leaving, but I did respond in a way that was consistent with how I have always faced risk. I could have begged them to stay, but that would have stolen my energy, and I needed every last bit of it to meet the deadline. I knew I would have to take the risk that I couldn't complete the task. I thought it was a smarter risk to do that than to waste an hour trying to convince them to step up to the plate. I was forced to choose between risks, and I chose the risk that gave me the most control over the circumstances.

I walked away with a lot of new skills I know I can use in any business, because some of the rules apply whether you're in real estate or electronics—work hard, think creatively, build teams, manage your time wisely, meet your deadlines, communicate.

There are two kinds of risk: risks you can prepare for and plan to address, and risks that simply come upon you without warning and leave you no choice other than to make a quick decision about how to face that risk. In each instance, knowledge is the key to success. The wider your knowledge, the more likely you will be able to make a plan to benefit from the risks you can see coming, and the more likely you'll react appropriately when risks come out of nowhere.

In the Pontiac task, I faced the second kind of risk, and I made the difficult, assertive choice. The choice paid off for me, but each time you run across a surprise risk, you face a new choice.

RECKLESS ENTREPRENEURS?

There's a difference between pushing your boundaries with an entrepreneurial eye and being a reckless risk junkie who lives for adrenaline. Surveys show that majority of Americans think entrepreneurs are wild risk takers, not careful businesspeople. Apparently, many business owners are buying into that image themselves, probably suffering from a post-dotcom hangover.

In his award-winning doctoral paper *Entrepreneurial Risk and Market Entry* (cowritten with Professor Anne Marie Knott of the University of Maryland), Wharton University Ph.D. Brian Wu says that American entrepreneurs are actually highly risk averse, but their inherent over-confidence cancels out their caution and compels them to take risks in building businesses. In a February 2005 interview with *BusinessWeek*, Wu says, "This disparity confronts two dimensions of uncertainty: one, the un-controllable risks or market uncertainty, and two, the uncertainty of ability. Entrepreneurs, like everybody else, hate uncontrollable risks, but on the other hand, they're overconfident in their own abilities—they think they can control their abilities in a random drawing of people. It's like the Lake Wobegon effect in assessing their position among peers. They think they're above the average."

Wu highlights the conflict between certainty about your own abili-ties—the one factor you can control—versus the fear of uncertain, uncon-trollable factors like market trends, and the different effects such levels of certainty exert on entrepreneurial behavior. "(The research) helps us to un-derstand the entry-pattern behavior of entrepreneurs across industries," he says. "We can see the dynamic of entrepreneurial behavior. When there's a high degree of uncontrollable uncertainty but a low degree of ability un-certainty, we won't see a sufficient level of entry into an industry. But if there's a high degree of ability uncertainty, we will see a sufficient amount of entrants because their overconfidence compensates for the uncontrol-lable risks."

Of course, it's one thing to take a wild idea and burn the midnight oil to turn it into a company and a fortune. But it's another to assume stupid, destructive risks out of overconfidence or a refusal to acknowledge reality. We've talked about serious planning and preparation as ways to reduce and manage risk, but you can't plan for incompetence. Exposing your company and yourself to risks that are outside your control, especially when a good lawyer or succession planner could protect you, is inexcusable.

Enthusiasm for risk and reckless confidence in their own abilities might help entrepreneurs get a business from the page to the marketplace, but when the same gung-ho attitude filters down into the culture of a growing company, it can be counterproductive, creating the risk of fraud or failure. Translation: although you can be a "cowboy" when you're angling for venture capital and throwing launch parties, you'd better be running the ranch when the time comes to sit in the CEO's chair.

Entrepreneurship in its pure form is noble and admirable. It's the force behind innovation, the force that has turned the United States into the world's primary economic engine. But what is entrepreneurship, and how does it differ from the blind, foolish risk taking that characterizes the worst in American business? How can you know the difference in your own ventures? To get to that answer, we first have to look at what entrepreneurs really do.

ENTREPRENEURS DEFINE WHAT'S POSSIBLE

KENDRA'S RULE OF RISK 9

Entrepreneurs prove that the new is possible.

There's always tremendous resistance, even ridicule, to any radically new idea. Philosopher Arthur Schopenhauer said, "All truth passes through three stages. First, it is ridiculed. Second, it is violently opposed. Third, it is accepted as self-evident." Playwright George Bernard Shaw backed him up with this observation: "All great truths begin as blasphemies." It's the entrepreneur's job to speak the blasphemies, to show us that things *can* be done in new ways, that automobiles can be built faster on an assembly line, with each person performing a single, specialized task, than one by one.

The greatest entrepreneurs, those I have the utmost respect for, are the people who have created something out of nothing, taken an idea and built it into a company of value that creates jobs, builds shareholder wealth, and contributes to society. I talked about Amazon.com's Jeff Bezos before, but there are many more people who are his kindred spirits:

— George Lucas turned his love of old movie serials into two multibillion-dollar film franchises *(Star Wars, Indiana Jones)* and the technology he developed to bring those films to the screen into a revolutionary special effects company, Industrial Light and Magic, that's changed how films are made.

— J.K. Rowling was a struggling single mother who wrote longhand for years in an Edinburgh coffeehouse, her sleeping child at her feet, crafting her stories of a boy wizard that would become the Harry Potter phenomenon.

— Major Dick Winters, leader of Easy Company, the 506th Regiment of the 101st Airborne Division, U.S. Army, parachuted behind enemy lines in Normandy on D-Day during World War II; returned to Lancaster, Pennsylvania, at the end of the war; became a livestock feed salesman; then started a business using the leftovers and by-products from the nearby Hershey chocolate factory. Quietly successful for years, Major Winters became a celebrity with the publication of Stephen Ambrose's *Band of Brothers* and spoke to audiences around the nation to remind them of the sacrifices made by soldiers during the war.

— Wally Amos grew up in his aunt Della's kitchen, baking cookies. After working as a theatrical agent (the first black agent at William Morris), he decided to open his own cookie business, Famous Amos, on Sunset Boulevard in Los Angeles in 1975. The shop was a success, but debts forced Amos to sell, and in an absurd twist he eventually lost control of the use of his own name as a brand. Undaunted and ever positive, he started a new company in Hawaii and continues to sell baked goods as well as publish four books and counting.

— Ruth Fertel came of age along the Mississippi River in Louisiana and worked to raise two young children as a single mother. Finally scraping together enough money to buy a small restaurant, she eventually turned her single diner into more than seventy-five Ruth's Chris Steak Houses, serving more than 15,000 steaks every day and earning her the unofficial title "First Lady of American Restaurants."

— Steve Jobs built the first Macintosh in his garage in the 1980s with Steve Wozniak and ushered in the PC era, withstood the assault of Microsoft, and has Apple Computer roaring back as the oracle of the digital lifestyle. Not to mention his hugely successful gamble in taking on the Disney animation juggernaut with Pixar, now recognized as the king of Hollywood digital animation studios.

— Ebby Halliday came to Dallas, Texas, in 1938 after working in the millinery business and found her way into real estate. In 1945, she was given the task of selling fifty-two experimental houses built out of cement. She sold the first two to gentlemen with shotguns over their shoulders, sold the entire development in a year, and an empire was born. Today, Ebby Halliday Realtors boasts 1,500 agents and is one of the twenty largest independent real estate firms in the nation. Ebby herself, at ninety-five, continues to oversee the business and is one of Texas's leading philanthropists.

— And, of course, there's Oprah, who went from a local talk show hostess to a billionaire media mogul who produces films, TV, and now Broadway shows, publishes a wildly successful magazine, has the power to turn an obscure novel into an overnight bestseller, and inspires women worldwide.

All these visionary entrepreneurs faced common barriers: entrenched cultures, disbelief in their ideas, lack of money, and fierce competition. But every entrepreneur battles those same foes and always will as long as there are entrepreneurs. It's the nature of the entrepreneur to see possibility where others see foolishness or, more often, nothing at all. That's why one of the most crucial assets for any entrepreneur is always an absolute, unshakable belief in his or her idea.

WHAT IS AN ENTREPRENEUR?

You've got the French definition. You know the common view that an entrepreneur is someone who starts a business. But if it were that simple, everybody would be self-employed. There's more to being an entrepreneur than that.

Samuel Zell, chairman of Equity Investments Group, the largest real estate investment trust in America, says that being an entrepreneur is lonely and often means "going right when everybody else is going left." According to Zell, entrepreneurs reject conventional wisdom, are able to seize opportunities with a sense of urgency, take risks, and "think outside the box." And they don't know the meaning of the word *failure*.

Delivering the University of Michigan Business School's forty-second annual Business Leadership Award lecture, Zell said, "An entrepreneur is somebody who doesn't have the word *failure* in his lexicon. Sometimes deals don't work out, but they never fail. Failure is accepting a resolution, when in fact a true entrepreneur uses his energy and self-confidence to live through difficult times. Failure is part of the process, but it isn't a conviction. It only restarts the process."

> **"Remember that great love and great achievements involve great risk."**
>
> **Unknown**

Earlier, we talked about the fact that the mention of failure gains traction only if you look at it as an ending, a reflection of some weakness or shortcoming in yourself. According to Zell, true entrepreneurs *never* take this view. They chalk it up to the vagaries of the marketplace, to a rival or to bad luck. They get up, make new plans, and jump back into the fight.

According to Geoffrey A. Timmons, in an article published by the

Harvard Business Review in 1979, true entrepreneurs share nine important qualities:

1. A high level of drive and energy

2. Enough self-confidence to take carefully calculated, moderate risks

3. A clear idea of money as a way of keeping score and as a means of generating more money

4. The ability to get others to work with you and for you productively

5. High but realistic, achievable goals

6. The belief that you can control your own destiny

7. Readiness to learn from your own mistakes and failures

8. A long-term vision of the future of your business

9. An intense competitive urge, with self-imposed standards

That sounds like a portrait of the classic Type A personality to me. Of course, I think this list leaves out the most important quality of all: *passion*. If you don't have a passion for what you're trying to build, you can't be an entrepreneur. And I don't mean a passion for making money; there's certainly nothing wrong with that, but it can't be your only motivator. You must have a fire in your belly for your idea, putting in long hours, giving up your home life, and spending your life savings, taking your product to the masses and creating something out of nothing. In its purest form, that's exactly what entrepreneurship is: creating something out of nothing by an act of pure will.

But for our purposes, take another look at the second characteristic:

calculated, moderate risks. That's what we're talking about here. True entrepreneurs are not gunslingers. They take smart risks tempered by planning, research, and knowledge of their marketplace. With these criteria in mind, you could argue that the would-be Internet barons of the 1990s dotcom boom were not entrepreneurs but gamblers—and amateur gamblers at that.

DANCE OF THE "WANTREPRENEURS"

I was still in college during the Internet business boom, but it was a heady time. I knew people, and knew people who knew people, who were starting Internet businesses all with the same goals: change the world, have a lot of fun doing it, and become a millionaire before age thirty.

Funny thing, though, it was always the same story. A couple of guys get together, come up with a vague business idea over coffee at Starbucks, flesh out what could loosely be called a business plan over midnight corn chips and tequila shots, and decide they want to be Internet moguls. They dress up and make the rounds to venture capitalists and "angel" investors to line up the money to launch their company. In those days, investment capital was practically falling out of the trees, especially along Sand Hill Road in Silicon Valley, where most of the big venture capital players were. You could waltz into a conference room with a PowerPoint presentation and a concept, and more often than not, waltz out with a commitment of $10 million. Such was the level of credulity in those innocent days.

Of course, then you had to launch and run your business. I heard firsthand accounts of would-be CEOs who didn't know what a profit-and-loss statement was, whose business model changed monthly, including one whose key technical asset was a dope-smoking former programmer for the porn industry whose only real skill was missing deadlines. It's hardly a surprise that 99 percent of these misbegotten companies went under within two or three years. What's more surprising is that anyone gave them money in the first place.

I get indignant when I hear stories like that, because they put entrepreneurship in a bad light. I'm proud that the businesses I've helped create are now creating jobs for other people, helping investors build their wealth, and helping contribute to the health of the local economy. That's a worthwhile enterprise. That's why the fly-by-night entrepreneurs who burned up billions in shareholder value make me furious. There are rules.

KENDRA'S RULE OF RISK 10

You don't put another person at risk without full disclosure.

The worst sin of the dotcom "wantrepreneurs" (I call them that because they want to be entrepreneurs but never will be) was that they took others down with them: venture capitalists, private investors, stockholders, employees whose stock options proved worthless. It's fine to take a long-shot risk on your own; as long as you go in with your eyes open, that's your decision. But if you're going to involve anyone else in your risk/reward situation, you'd better damn well let them know the risks—the real risks—before you do.

The difference between smart risk and foolish risk is clear in those now-dead Internet businesses. The smart risk lay in starting a business based on an idea and hard work, and in spending perhaps years trying to convince people to invest in it. Entrepreneurs take risks they can exercise some control over, wise risks. But when the self-styled moguls started their companies with friends and hangers-on and policies that were more about keg parties than marketing strategies, they introduced stupid, unnecessary, uncontrollable risk into their businesses. No real entrepreneur does that. And because they usually didn't disclose that they had no idea what they were doing, they put investors and many other people at risk without their consent. In my book, that's called theft. Risk is a *choice*, and everybody should have all the information they need to make a clear-eyed choice about whether to accept the risk or not.

Entrepreneurs live by that rule. "Wantrepreneurs" don't.

THE SELF-EMPLOYED SHALL INHERIT THE EARTH

If you read the many books about wealth and wealth building such as *The Millionaire Next Door* by Thomas J. Stanley and William D. Danko, one of the key principles most of them talk about is that to be a millionaire, you must own your own business. I don't happen to agree with that, since in my professional experience you can become a millionaire by investing wisely in real estate, and I'm going to show you the basics of doing that in this book. But their point is a good one. The more control you have over your financial destiny and the growth of your income, the better your odds of becoming wealthy.

But where is the line between being self-employed and being an entrepreneur? There are millions of people around the country working for themselves as writers, photographers, day care providers, car detailers, you name it. If we agree that any entrepreneur is someone who brings a new idea to market, then you can't really argue that these people are entrepreneurs. They're sole proprietors. But they do share many of the same characteristics as the true entrepreneur, including their approach to risk.

"Never measure the height of a mountain until you have reached the top. Then you will see how low it was."

**Dag Hammarskjold,
Former UN Secretary-General,
Markings (Knopf, 1964)**

In fact, when you think about it, becoming self-employed is a lot riskier and scarier than being an entrepreneur. If you leave your job as a designer at an advertising agency to start your own design shop, you're not going to venture capitalists with your hat in your hand like Oliver Twist, asking for just a little more money. As a self-employed sole proprietor, you might have two or three clients, but otherwise you're turning your back on a steady paycheck and trying to bootstrap your one-person company into a going concern. That's real risk: giving up a sure thing for something that's completely dependent on your wits, your skills, and your hard work, and which still fails four times out of five. No wonder most people who say, "I've always wanted to start my own business" never do.

Self-employed people share other qualities with company-building entrepreneurs, too: a desire for independence, a self-starter quality that gets them moving without a boss telling them to, and a mindset that sees the unknown as a challenge, not as something to fear. But I think the factory they both have most in common is one that you'll see in all successful people: the drive for control of their future. The self-employer and the entrepreneur both hate the idea of their earning potential and advancement being dependent on some corporate bureaucrat. There's a faint, healthy arrogance to them, a sense of "I can do better than these jokers." I believe that desire for self-determination is crucial and sets self-employed and entrepreneurial people apart from the rest of the population. They're not the type to sit back and accept an unhappy situation or to let someone else cash in on a potential opportunity.

SELF-EMPLOYED TO ENTREPRENEURIAL

Then there's the obvious connection between the two: folks who start out as self-employed one-person shows in tiny offices sometimes end up launching and running huge companies. It's a natural progression. If you're savvy and driven enough to quit a job and stand or fall on your own merits, you're probably the type of person who's going to become bored working alone for the rest of her life, doing the same thing. You're likely, at some point, to want to hire people. To start a company. To build something bigger, a legacy you can sell or pass on to your kids.

That's precisely how many multigeneration businesses get started. You've never heard of them, but they've been going for decades because Grandpa came from the old country and after a few years laying bricks decided he could run a contracting business as well as the next guy. Eventually, he became an entrepreneur, though that was the farthest thing from his mind going in.

COULD YOU BE SELF-EMPLOYED?

I doubt there's anyone in the American workforce who hasn't, at one time or another, particularly after a really lousy week at the office, said, "You know, I should just start my own business." You've probably said it. But could you? Take this informal quiz to see if you have what it takes:

SELF-EMPLOYMENT SUITABILITY TEST

1. Can you handle having no steady, predictable income?

2. Do you love the idea of being in control of your time?

3. Can you be the name on the door and the one everybody comes to with complaints or problems?

4. Can you get out and sell?

5. Do you know what it takes to market yourself and bring in business?

6. Do you have the discipline to work at home when you'd rather be watching TV or riding your bike?

7. Do uncertainty and possibility stimulate you?

If you were able to answer "Yes" to all the questions, you're ideally suited to be self-employed, so if you're not, why not? What's stopping you? If you answered "No" to even one, you're probably not ready. It takes a very specific type of personality to be self-employed, one that's just as much about long hours and discipline as it is about talent.

But if you are right for it, you'll enjoy the greatest benefit there is: the knowledge that your wealth is limited only by your skill, your willingness to work hard, and your ability to locate opportunities and take the risks to make them pay off.

THE REGULAR PAYCHECK TORTURE

Drip, drip, drip. No doubt you've heard of the Chinese water torture, gradually dripping its victims into madness, one drop at a time. But I'm talking about American regular paycheck torture, which strips its victims of all their risk-taking spirit and leaves them complacent, falsely secure, and forever unable to change their lot in life.

When I left *Capture Life* to work with Charles at MyHouse, I was nervous about going into sales. I had an image in my mind of sleazy car salesmen in checkered sport coats and loud ties; sales seemed dirty to me, somehow. But what I think I was really feeling was the uneasiness that comes with making a living in a pay-for-performance job. Most people draw a paycheck every two weeks for a preset amount; whether they excel at their job or spend their time yakking with friends on the phone and answering Internet personals, they're paid the same. They never have to worry about making the rent or the car payment, because their earnings are completely predictable. They get lazy, secure, satisfied with the status quo. The regular paycheck can lull you into a coma that doesn't break until retirement age.

The big problem with depending on a preset paycheck is that someone else is determining your worth. You have little or nothing to say about what you earn, which, if your work is making huge bucks for your employer—say, you're a software programmer for Microsoft—is fundamentally unfair. The other big problem with the regular paycheck is that it provides no motivation. Everyone on the planet needs to be motivated by something—passion, danger, adrenaline, greed, you name it. But when you don't have a hand in determining the reward for your work, where's your motivation? If it's fear of losing your job, get out now! Sure, some people are motivated by a desire to do their best or a goal of advancement, but most of us want to see our reward in dollars and cents.

Then take the entrepreneur, hanging everything out on the edge, dependent on his or her wits, work, and persistence to make a living. That's the potential that got me into sales despite my fears—the knowledge that eventually, the only limit that would be placed on my income would be how hard I worked and how smart I was. That's positive motivation, which is why all salespeople are entrepreneurs, even if they work for a company for a small base salary plus commissions. Getting paid only if you perform is the best way to motivate yourself to perform. Starvation and foreclosure are worth a thousand cheerleading speeches from motivational speakers.

BECOME ENTREPRENEURIAL

So does this mean that you should dump your salaried job for a pay-for-performance gig? Or that if you stay in your salaried job, you're doomed to a life of mediocrity? No and no. Obviously, for some people, the predictability of a regular paycheck is important—people with children, folks in debt, and so on. But, ultimately, I believe that if you're going to reach your full financial and career potential, yes, you must work for yourself or start your own business. We've seen over the last few decades that people who accumulate a net worth of more than $1 million tend to own their own businesses. Becoming an entrepreneur gives you the freedom of self-determination—no one but you gets to decide what you can make. You're free to work as hard and long as you like or to balance work and lifestyle in any way you see fit. If you have a great idea and a way to bring it to market, you can get rich. Being an entrepreneur is all about freedom, the freedom to live, earn, and work as you choose.

That said, many people fear becoming entrepreneurs. It's the same fear that keeps them from going into pay-for-performance jobs like sales: the fear that they aren't good enough, that they can't cut it. That's natural, but you can't let it control you. I made nothing during my first six months in real estate, but I didn't let that discourage me. I knew I was doing the right thing and that it would pay off. I had faith that I was good enough and that

I would succeed. If your fear of failure is keeping you dependent on the safety net of a regular paycheck when you'd rather be testing your limits, ask yourself, "Why? What have I got to lose?"

But let's say that your desire for risk has nothing to do with your career. Maybe it's all about music or art or political activism. That doesn't mean you have to be stuck in a boring job, too. It's possible to be entrepreneurial in a job working for someone else. You can bring new ideas to light and create new opportunities or turn yourself into a leader. Even within the confines of a corporate job, you can practice entrepreneurship by freeing your creativity and challenging yourself. That way, you have the best of both worlds: a reliable income plus the stimulation and growth that comes with risk.

MY OWN ENTREPRENEURIAL SIDE

I've always been entrepreneurial. If I hadn't been, I wouldn't have had the audacity to launch *Capture Life* magazine right out of college, and I wouldn't have walked into the meat grinder as editor-in-chief. Of course, it was an incredible experience. But that entrepreneurial spirit came in part from my upbringing, and from my dad, Navy aviator Captain John Todd. He always told me that I could do anything. I believed him. Self-confidence was part of my life growing up, and it has carried over into everything I've done as an adult. My mom, Cheryl, pushed me to strive for excellence and didn't punish me when I made mistakes. In our society we are graded on everything, and when you take a test in school and you're wrong, your grade drops. But learning from mistakes in business is important. Mom encouraged me to learn from my mistakes.

After Charles successfully recruited me to join MyHouse, my entrepreneurial energies were channeled in a different direction. Instead of being the captain of my own ship, I was sharing the leadership role with a man who is one of the most entrepreneurial I've ever known. I was also dealing with the reality of any new business: it takes time to establish yourself. Like I said, I didn't make a cent in my first six months. Not that I had been swimming in Dom Perignon at the magazine, but now I was earning zero, and it was humbling. But gradually, I learned the tricks of the trade, made key contacts, closed some deals, and I was off and running.

In helping to run and grow MyHouseRE.com, I quickly found myself practicing two levels of entrepreneurship: as the architect of a company that had been a one-man show but was growing with me as president, and as a sort of entrepreneur-by-proxy for our clients. With the first, I'm engaged in the types of activities you'd expect from an executive in a small but growing firm—developing new strategies, marketing, networking, hiring and firing staff, and handling the endless small details that make a business run.

But with the second, I'm engaged in something that's incredibly stimulating. Our clients are not, by and large, entrepreneurs. They are people who have a little money to invest and a desire to build wealth in a way that minimizes their risk. It's my job as their proxy to think like an entrepreneur on their behalf—to ferret out opportunities, to ask hard questions, and to be ready to act fast when the conditions look right. The stakes are higher than just me; there are others involved. That changes things. I'm a survivor; I can land on my feet no matter what comes my way. My limitations aren't what I thought they were. If something goes bad, I have no doubt I will bounce back.

There's no guarantee that the people MyHouseRE.com matches with investments are the same way. Few people are. If I make a misjudgment and guide my clients into a poor risk that costs them big money, it's likely that they're going to have a tough time bouncing back. It's going to be a major blow to them, and they might never be able to convince themselves to invest again. That's the responsibility on my shoulders. And you know what? It's sharpened my entrepreneurial eye, made me more determined than ever to find ways to minimize risk, to stick to the MyHouse real estate success formula, and to create something from nothing for our clients. It's made me a better, more conscientious, more effective entrepreneur. I can honestly say I have never had a client walk away from a deal I put together without making money.

ENTREPRENEURS CAN MAKE A DIFFERENCE

No business opportunity means more to me than having a platform to make a difference in people's lives. For me, it's never just about the money. It can't be. That's not enough of a reason to get up in the morning and work as hard as I do. It's got to be something more.

I take the same approach toward my life as an entrepreneur. Whether it's with MyHouseRE.com or with this book and the other projects I've been working on, I have three goals:

1. Have a great time learning amazing new things.

2. Lay the groundwork for future successes.

3. Touch people in a meaningful, positive way.

If I do these things and follow my formula, wealth is inevitable.

As an entrepreneur, I'm not limited by other people's ideas of what can be done. As travel author Bill Bryson once said memorably, I'm radiant with ignorance. There's no one to tell me what can't be done, so I find a way to do it. That freedom allows me, in my work as a real estate professional, to do more than sell condos. I'm able to craft opportunities out of thin air that build wealth and security for people, help developers restore aging communities, give people affordable places to live, and sustain local economies in Florida and elsewhere. I do a lot of good with my entrepreneurial fire.

If you have that fire in you, how would you use it to do well *and* do good?

THINK LIKE AN ENTREPRENEUR

There is an entrepreneur mentality, or EM. And contrary to what you might think, it's not built around risk. Risk is a major component in any venture, but true entrepreneurs don't think about risk as a part of their project. It's an outside element to be dealt with, like the weather. It can be prepared for and endured, but it's not going to stop them.

This book is focused on what you can do to take risks, transform your life, and ultimately create wealth. One of the best ways to do that is to take careful, wise risks as an entrepreneur. But first you've got to have your EM in place. As *Chicken Soup for the Soul* cocreator Mark Victor Hansen says, entrepreneurship is a state of mind, one that can change the world if used in the right way.

So what is the entrepreneur mentality? It has a number of components:

"Builder's Eye"

This is the most important part of the EM. Charles has this in abundance. From his perspective on the world, if there's a need that's not being met, he feels it's his duty is to build something from nothing to meet that need. That's where MyHouseRE.com came from. That's where our lending company, United Mutual Lending, came from. He's been such an amazing teacher and partner.

Entrepreneurs have the builder's eye. It's genetic. They can't help themselves. When most folks see an unmet need in the marketplace, they might not even notice it. If they do, they shake their heads and say, "That's too bad." That's it. Not the one with the builder's eye: he or she looks and says, "I could start a company that would take care of that." Then the entrepreneur runs back to his or her office, adrenaline pumping, to do research on the Internet and find out if anyone else has already come up with the idea. If not, you can bet by the end of the day there will be a website and a company name already registered, and a new company will be gestating. Congratulations, it's an LLC (limited liability company)!

Do you have the eye? Have you ever found yourself mapping out a company on a napkin after seeing a problem that needed solving? You're an entrepreneur in the making.

EXAMPLE: I have the builder's eye. In 2003 I bought a real estate investment before I ever bought a home for myself. I found a neighborhood that had really nice homes, but they were selling at a price point that was suppressed compared to everything I had seen in the county. I saw this immediately. When you talk about comps (comparably priced homes used in appraisals), you typically use properties in same area. Well, I was buying the house for $201,000, which was $7,000 higher than the highest sale ever in the neighborhood. Most people would have said I was crazy (in fact, Charles did), but I knew the entire neighborhood was priced at about $70,000 less than anything else in Palm Beach County. Within eight months of closing, the entire area shot up in line with rest of the region. My house was worth $320,000 a year later and it's worth $380,000 now. That's paper wealth I can use to acquire more property, or if I want to I can cash out and turn my equity into profit. What you choose to do all depends on what you're comfortable with and what your goals are.

When you start to become more familiar with surroundings, you know a deal when you hear the price and see the location of the property. That's how you develop the builder's eye. We'll talk in more detail about how to use the paper wealth of equity to build your million-dollar net worth in chapter 9.

Belief

I spoke earlier about passion. It's important. But it's not all you need. An entrepreneur has to believe in the basic *rightness* of an idea—that even though the naysayers claim it will never work, it can and will work, given enough time and dedication. This is different from passion (you need both)—passion fuels your actions, but belief *guides* them.

A successful entrepreneur needs belief that approaches pig-headedness to deal with opposition—and you will face opposition. Think again of Amazon.com. The wolves were at the door of that company more times than I can count, and each time Jeff Bezos stayed the course. He believed that his business model would be a success. Sure, he was supported with market research and a load of facts telling him it *could* succeed, but that's not the same thing as believing it *will.* In the face of all the people telling you your idea is silly, it will never work, you'll lose everything, you need to believe to keep going. You've got to believe that your risk is still worthwhile.

Can belief cross over into blindness? Sure, if your belief contradicts facts that are obvious to anyone else, then you've drunk the Kool-Aid. That's when someone you trust needs to take you aside and tell you some hard truths. Or perhaps you need to fail spectacularly to learn. That's what it takes for some people. Either way, be cautious; make sure that your belief is based on reality. Wishful thinking is not a success strategy.

EXAMPLE: Real estate is always changing. If rates go up another 2 or 3 percent, the housing craze is going to slow down. What will go up are short sales and foreclosures, the bank-owned (or REO, for real estate owned) properties. Charles is fearless in his belief that you have to be proactive in getting into these opportunities before the herd. You've got to have the connections with the banks and lenders. You've got to be fluid. You have to be a futurist and figure out the next market. He's already got us thinking about investing in Las Vegas gaming companies like Boyd Gaming and in water projects to serve that fast-growing market. Once you figure out where the market is going, you need an absolute belief that getting into it is the right thing to do.

Mission

This ties into what I said about doing good. If you see an unmet need and have an idea to meet it, have a mission in mind. Most great entrepreneurs don't just start companies, they take on causes. Sometimes, company and cause are one and the same, as with Habitat for Humanity. I believe in the power of entrepreneurs to create solutions and change the world, but to do that you've got to have a mission. I define it as a vision for the effect you would like to have on society with what you create.

It doesn't have to be big, just sincere. It also doesn't have to be heart-wrenching and touchy-feely. If you want to build a website that makes it easier for parents to find educational programming for their kids, great. If you're starting a clothing company and trying to use all recycled materials to grow that market, wonderful. If you just want to run your own financial planning firm and get rich while helping people build their retirement nest egg, that's awesome. But have a destination in mind for what you build, not just a product, a name, and a logo.

And if your company takes off and becomes successful, adjust your mission as you grow. When you're small it makes sense to work with a local charity to repair discarded bikes for poor kids. But when you're a $250 million corporation, you should be raising money for something like building decent roads in impoverished African villages. As what you've built changes, so should your mission.

EXAMPLE: There are many ways to do well and do good. One is simply by acting with integrity at all times. Charles says that one of the reasons developers love to work with us is that no matter what's happening, we tell them the truth. As he likes to say, "I could lose money just by telling the truth. But you don't have time for games. You owe your business partners the truth, even if it's not what they want to hear."

Another example: As this book was being finalized, we had a client with $22,000 deposited on a property, and they had passed the fifteen-day period, when they could have backed out of the deal. Now they had to get all the paperwork done, but they wouldn't do it. They had a very laissez-faire attitude; they would call and leave messages and claim they were trying, but they wouldn't pull the trigger. Normally, we'll fire a client like that. But Charles didn't. He went to the developer and cashed in a few favors, and the developer was gracious enough to let the couple back out and get their money back. Why? Because you deal with people fairly and you don't burn bridges. That's just the right way to do business.

But I think our mission can be summed up in how we give back to the community. I put a post on KatrinaHousing.org and we found a family—a husband, wife, and eighteen-month-old girl from LaPlace, Louisiana, right outside New Orleans—who had lost everything in Hurricane Katrina. We are sponsoring them and footing all their bills until they can get back on their feet. Their house was looted and the husband's place of work destroyed. We thought that, instead of giving money to far-off charities, we could make a more immediate impact by providing immediate relief to one family. Therefore, we have dedicated all of our resources to them. It's costing me thousands of dollars to house them in one of my properties, because I still have my mortgage, taxes, and all the bills to cover, with no rental income. I've given them new appliances, food, furniture, and more. But it feels good to help people. When you're as fortunate as we've been, it's your duty to aid those in need. That's what really gives the work Charles and I do meaning. It makes it about more than making money.

Market Smarts

A fantastic idea for a product or service isn't much good if you don't know how to bring it to market. You've got to have some basic market and business skills, or partner with someone who does. This is where the "wantrepreneurs" fell short. They may have known technology, but they didn't know marketing or customer service from a hole in the ground. Do your homework. Talk to people who have run successful companies and find out what they're doing right.

Some of the topics any aspiring entrepreneur should become knowledgeable in*:

— Accounting

— Business plans

— Market research

— Customer relationships

---

* At the back of the book, in the Resources section, you'll find some handy reference sources with information about these topics.

— Business technology

— Business loans

— Sales

— Distribution

— Basic business law

— Personnel management

Fortunately, if you have a few good people on your team with a wide range of skills, you can learn as you go, hopefully not making any catastrophic mistakes along the way. But even if you're partnered with the best and the brightest, it's in your best interest to get a grounding in all the core disciplines of running a business. After all, if a ship runs aground, the captain is at fault no matter who's at the wheel.

EXAMPLE: If you don't have the skills, surround yourself with people who do. When I ran *Capture Life,* I didn't know anything about sales, but I recognized the importance of building trust. We hired a girl, Cari Cascio, to run the sales department. Let me tell you, if you can sell a one-page glossy ad in a magazine with no mockup of the first issue, you can sell anything. I watched this girl create a level of trust with advertisers until they wanted to do business with her because they liked her. Successful salespeople sell themselves before they sell anyone else. I would rather hire someone with raw talent and no skills but with great integrity because I can train them in the skills I need. Cari sold about $18,000 in advertising for that first issue on charm and smarts alone. That's what I mean by surrounding yourself with the best people.

Creative Destruction

Genuine entrepreneurs love creative destruction. You'll have to embrace it to be truly successful. Creative destruction means that you're always discarding what's old for what's new and better. You're a master at disrupting the status quo. You have no sacred cows; you can't afford them. Creative destruction means when the electric typewriter comes along, manual typewriters are instantly sold to the used office equipment store. When computers with word processing software come along, electric typewriters get mothballed. And on and on.

To develop your EM, you need to embrace creative destruction, to revel in it. You need to savor the thrill of coming up with something new that turns the marketplace upside down, even if it also hurts an existing product or company that you like. Entrepreneurs get a visceral charge out of creating anything new, even if it's just a business plan. If you know what that feels like, you're an entrepreneur in training already.

EXAMPLE: You still have to be willing to turn your back on what used to work but doesn't work any longer. Allow no sacred cows to trample your business. A couple of years ago, the best way to make the best returns in real estate was preforeclosures, buying properties for seventy cents on the dollar before the lender could swoop down. Then new construction fell off because of the cost of fuel and building materials and everybody started getting into preforeclosures. Now the competition is swarming. Once upon a time, the county would auction foreclosed properties on the courthouse steps and you could get great deals. Now, the auctions are ending $40,000 or $50,000 *above* market value. The market has changed again, and a lot of people are having trouble embracing the changes. But the people like Charles and me, who realized there was more money in conversions and preconstruction, are doing well. People who fought change have had increased competition and lower profits. You have to grow into being comfortable with change. I'm a person who never liked change. But I also knew learning to "surf" change was important if I was going to evolve. I have a fear of heights, but I'm the first person to get into the front car of the rollercoaster, because I know how important it is to overcome fear. You've got to know when it's time to let something go and embrace the new.

Observation

To be a successful entrepreneur is to be obsessed with what's happening in your market, your industry, your culture. Observing is a method of reducing risk, and it begins even before you open the doors to your spanking new business. Once you have your idea, you've got to watch the market like a hawk. Is anyone doing anything like it? Is the culture changing, which will change demand? Is an existing company making noises that suggest they might want to buy your idea?

Don't become paranoid, but do become hyperaware. Smart entrepreneurs are always observing the marketplace for signs of what's to come, so they can make course corrections in their own businesses. Cultivate sources—business contacts, websites, trade publications, as well as mainstream newspapers and magazines. Spend a few hours each week monitoring what's happening in all the segments of your world that affect your business.

Do you have to be an obsessive, borderline delusional, goal-driven, problem-solving market scholar to be a successful entrepreneur? Pretty much, yeah. The funny thing is, there are a lot of people out there with all these qualities at various levels. They're not all experts, so they often team up. You might be one of them.

When I got into real estate, I read all the local papers, *Forbes, Kiplinger's,* and the like, but there were two books I absorbed that taught me priceless lessons. The first was *Rich Dad, Poor Dad,* by Robert Kiyosaki. It completely changed my outlook. It was an introduction to financial intelligence and taking control of life instead of being stuck on the treadmill of working for someone else and living paycheck to paycheck. The other book that changed my life was *The E-Myth,* by Michael Gerber. This book opened my eyes to the misconceptions about running a business, and helped me understand that if I wanted to be truly successful, I had to have both technical skills and the vision of an entrepreneur. I also read books by Russ Whitney, like *The Millionaire Real Estate Mentor,* that taught me how to approach the mental side of my profession. I highly recommend all those books.

However, let me warn you. Often, people new to an industry will dive into books, getting the big concepts while ignoring the basics. That's a mistake. Master the nuts and bolts first. You're going to learn the details while you're out there doing deals, making investments, and talking to people. People tell me, "I haven't read enough." Put down the books and get out there and make deals. No one is going to hand you all the secrets to becoming a millionaire in ten chapters. I can't do it in this book and I'm not even going to try.

KENDRA'S RULE OF RISK 11

Don't expect to find the tricks of the trade in a book. Look at yourself in the mirror, learn the basics, accept a degree of risk, then get out and do it.

WHAT MAKES ENTREPRENEURIAL RISK DIFFERENT

I've written about a lot of kinds of risk, and how risk is an inseparable aspect of being an entrepreneur. If you venture into new territory and create something that hasn't been seen before, there's risk involved. I've written about the fact that, contrary to the popular image, entrepreneurs aren't wild-haired base jumpers who take crazy risks for the buzz. They take calculated, moderate risks if they take them at all.

But lots of people take calculated and moderate risks who aren't entrepreneurs. They plan and prepare and mitigate, but they're not entrepreneurs. So what makes entrepreneurial risk different from any other kind?

KENDRA'S RULE OF RISK 12

Entrepreneurial risk is energy: it gets used up and needs to be replenished.

Stick with me and I'll explain. Entrepreneurs take risks with the interest of building something for the long term, a company that might last for decades. Over time, if they're smart and don't introduce unnecessary risk into their business through negligence or recklessness, the level of risk decreases. They gain market share. Their brand grows. They become more profitable. Their risk tank runs low, which is a bad thing. You see, risk is the energy source for any business. Foolish risks hurt businesses, but wise, bold, planned risks spark growth and innovation. Once a company's level of that kind of risk drops too low, they need to increase it, take new risks. Businesses need smart risk like a car needs gasoline. The best *Fortune* 500 and 1000 corporations spend a great deal of time, effort, and money each year fostering entrepreneurship and invention among their employees:

— A great example is 3M, where a long-standing tradition encourages personnel to develop their own ideas. Out of such visionary policies come products like Post-It Notes, which have sold billions of units around the world, been featured at New York's Museum of Modern Art, and, according to 3M, had reached $1 billion in sales back in 1998.

— Apple's Steve Jobs said in 2001 when the post-Internet boom slump threatened the computer industry, "We're going to innovate our way out of this." The result was the iPod, which has created entirely new product lines and spawned new terms such as "podcasting," and currently owns a whopping 82 percent of the U.S. retail market for portable digital music players, generating $249 million in sales in the third quarter of 2005.

— Lewis S. Ranieri joined Salomon Brothers in the late 1970s and quickly created the concept of "securitization," wherein mortgages are converted into bonds that can be sold anywhere around the globe. The move galvanized the home-buying market, reducing costs and creating trillions in new wealth for homeowners and investors.

— Pierre Omidyar spent Labor Day weekend of 1995 programming a new website that he called Auction Web. His concept: to allow individuals to buy, sell, and trade goods online and cut out the corporate middlemen. Today, that website is called eBay, which posted gross revenues in 2004 of nearly $3 billion and has enabled hundreds of thousands of online entrepreneurs to make a living buying and selling a galaxy of items.

That's the difference between entrepreneurial risk and other kinds: you don't want to let your risk level get too low. That's how you become a stolid, stagnant company that can't change with the times. You always want to be looking for the strongest source of wind, even if it's unpredictable. Like a sailor tacking about for the best breeze, there's a chance that a sudden gust will grab you and take you somewhere unexpected, even hazardous. But if you trust your skills, you know you can handle the wind, and the ride can take you to even more rewarding destinations. Risk for businesses is like wind for sailors: a source of power and progress, something you can never stop chasing.

REMAKE YOURSELF AS AN ENTREPRENEUR

Before we finish with our chapter on entrepreneurship and the things that make it thrilling and unique, let's take a look at what you can do to reinvent yourself as an entrepreneur.

Is it that easy? Can you just say "I'm an entrepreneur"? Yes. How do you think the rest of them do it? There's no school that teaches you how to do it. There are plenty of suits with MBAs who couldn't launch a company on a shoestring if their lives depended on it. But you can . . . if you retrace these steps, develop your EM, and follow your passion.

Step 1: Find That Unmet Need

You can swim a lot faster downstream than upstream. The risk of drowning is less, too. Finding the unmet need is simply a matter of looking at a market that you know well—retail business, for instance—and asking yourself, "What's not being done for the customer that should be done?" It might not come to you right away; sometimes the unmet need isn't that obvious. That's why you want to wear your entrepreneur hat at all times: you might stumble on a situation where the unmet need hits you like a bolt of lightning. In fact, that's often how it happens. Keep a pad and pen with you at all times to write down your inspiration and you're on your way.

Step 2: Come Up With a Novel Solution

Copycats go broke. Sometimes they get sued, but more often they just bleed cash until they expire, wounded from going up against a rival who's been doing exactly what they do but longer and probably better. Your solution to the unmet need should be original and innovative—something that no one has seen, no one has been able to figure out how to make work, or an improved version of an existing idea.

Notice that a novel solution doesn't necessarily mean a totally new idea. How many times have you seen this dynamic: one company pioneers an idea, critics call it brilliant, but the market isn't ready for it and they eventually go under. Then a new company comes along a couple of years later, learns from the first company's mistakes, puts out the same product, only better, and becomes a huge success. Take the condominium conversion market in South Florida, considered the conversion capital. Many developers resisted it, and most of the initial projects were small. Then players like SunVest Resorts and Tarragon Corporation got involved and streamlined the model: avoid bad blood by giving renters a priority option to purchase units, presell units during conversion, and add top-quality amenities. The result: a thriving industry in which the value of apartments sold to become condos in 2005 was $22.6 billion, according to Real Capital Analytics.

Whatever your innovation, you might be tempted to trademark it or patent it. Check into it (or better yet, have your lawyer do it), but don't spend a ton of time on it. The time you spend filling out trademark forms would be better spent on your business plan and marketing.

Step 3: Find a Partner(s)

You've read the laundry list of qualities I've told you a great entrepreneur needs. Do you have all of them at a high level? Of course not. Nobody does. That's why entrepreneurs partner when they launch new ventures. Bill Gates and Paul Allen. Steve Jobs and Steve Wozniak. Spielberg, Katzenberg, and Geffen at Dreamworks. And on and on. Partnering brings more of the pieces of the entrepreneurial puzzle together. It also takes the pressure off you to do everything. You can be the creative genius while one partner is the money mind, and another is the marketing guru. There is strength in numbers.

How do you find partners? How do you meet people? Chances are you already know some people who could bring to the table some of the attributes you're missing. If not, try networking websites like Media Bistro, Ryze, and Meetup. Read the business and venture capital press (such as *Funding Post, Venture Capital Journal,* and the family of newsletters at www.venturewire.com) for news about people who have the skills you need. Contact editors and publish an article about your idea (going light on the details) in your local newspaper's business section, your regional business journal, or a local entrepreneurship website, and see who comes to you. Pull together a small team with complementary skill sets.

One warning: do *not* partner with friends just because they're friends. Friends sometimes feel a sense of entitlement, as if they shouldn't have to work hard or produce because you grew up together. Hiring friends is a great way to ruin friendships and harm your business in the bargain.

Step 4: Plan

As I've said, planning reduces your risk, and in this case we're talking about a business plan. You've heard about them, but they're not as complicated as you might think. Sit down and map out:

— What your product or service is

— Who your market is

— How your company will be structured

— How you'll fund the launch

— Who your competition is and what their strengths and weaknesses are

— How you will produce your product

— How you will sell it

— How you will market it

— How much revenue you expect to earn and when you expect to be profitable

That's the basic skeleton. You can find lots of examples on the Web. Your own business is your hedge against risk, your insurance against the unpredictable. With it, you still have plenty of risks, but they're more manageable.

Step 5: Commit

You might expect this step to be "Get money." That's important, but not as important as making a total commitment to making your idea work. Finding partners? Writing a business plan? Thinking about how rich your idea will make you? Those are all fun. But hitting the streets to find investors and burning the midnight oil to make your launch date, that's work. You're going to hit walls. You're going to run up against what you think are your limitations, just as I did. You're going to get discouraged. You're going to want to throw in the towel, kiss off the risk, and go back to a nine-to-five job.

The only thing that stops you is your commitment and that of your partners. Write it down and make it an oath if you need to, but make it. Remember it when things get rough. They will get better. Remember, a true entrepreneur never fails, just takes the lessons learned, tries again, and comes back better.

6.

HOW TO BECOME A "RISK DIVER"

"To dare every day to be irreverent and bold. To dare to preserve the randomness of mind which in children produces strange and wonderful new thoughts and forms. To continually scramble the familiar and bring the old into new juxtaposition."

GORDON WEBBER, VICE PRESIDENT, BENTON & BOWLES, *ADVERTISING AGE*, OCTOBER 31, 1960

I've never done it, but I love the idea of skydiving. Raymond Young coined the term in the 1950s, when a surplus of parachutes left over from World War II—and a surfeit of ex-paratroopers and aviators still craving something of the thrills they saw during their training drops and military campaigns—led to an entirely new industry: people jumping out of planes for fun. But it's more than the name. The concept is electrifying: jumping out of an aircraft flying at 10,000 feet (a terrifying prospect even for the most prepared novice), surrendering to the clutch of gravity as you free-fall, watching the earth unfold below you like a quilt being shaken out onto a bed. Then at just the right time, you pull your ripcord and feel the chute stream into the air above you, burst open like a flower, and slow you from a lethal plunge to a pleasant, swinging descent. You guide yourself down, hit the landing zone, and voilà! You've gone from total safety to mortal danger to absolute wonder to standing on terra firma as if nothing had happened. Incredible.

But what really appeals to me about skydiving is that it's the most perfect metaphor for approaching a really scary risk that rips you far outside your comfort zone. The act of jumping out of a perfectly functional plane is, of course, totally crazy on the surface. But you minimize that risk with training, planning, mentoring, and high-quality equipment. The risk is still high—something could go wrong—but you've made it manageable. All the time, it takes a certain "go for it" mindset to be able to skydive at all. It's thrill, risk, preparation and exhilarating payoff all rolled into one. That's why it's so addictive for so many people.

THE RIGHT MIX OF HEAD AND GUT

Smart risk taking is exactly the same as safe skydiving. The risk is exciting, but you don't jump into it without preparation and planning to reduce the risks. You act boldly, but not overaggressively or foolishly. With that approach, both jumping out of a plane and developing your own business should be more thrilling than frightening. And you'll want to do both again and again.

One of the key parts of becoming a successful risk diver is finding the right balance between your gut, which is screaming, *"Go for it!"* and your head, which is saying, *"Stop. Think about what you're doing."* A skydiver who hasn't taken the trouble to pack her chute properly doesn't just run the risk that it won't open and she'll die; terror will also ruin the exhilaration of the free-fall, which is the whole point of skydiving in the first place. In the same way, if you don't listen to your gut, you'll never make the jump into a new business venture and leave that comfort zone, but if all you listen to is your gut, odds are you'll come limping back bruised and regretful, feeling foolish, and a lot poorer into the bargain.

If your big risk is becoming a major investor in a new company (what's commonly called an "angel"), you should do your due diligence: research, talking to the top managers, looking over the business plan, and so on. If you don't, if you simply hand over your $500,000 and hold on for the ride, you're doing what plenty of stupid investors did during the dotcom days—throwing away a hell of a lot of money for what will probably turn out to be nothing more than an emotional rush.

EXAMPLE: A couple of years ago, Charles didn't trust his gut and lost out on what would have been the biggest deal of his career. A guy came to him, drove him out to some farmland, and told him he had the option on the land and that developers were planning to build a mall on it. He asked Charles to partner with him in "flipping" the option—the right to purchase—to the developers. Instead of doing his due diligence and finding out about the development prospects, Charles looked around at the cows and farmland and said, "No thanks." Well, shortly after that, residential developers came in and built Wellington, one of the wealthiest areas in Palm Beach County, where the homes sell for up to $3 million. And on that land that Charles passed on was recently built the Mall at Wellington Green, a preposterously opulent shopping center. Charles still kicks himself to this day; for a comparatively small investment, he could have made millions selling the land to the mall developers. It would have been the biggest deal of his career. Funny thing, it's made him a smarter evaluator of risk. He knows now that if the reward looks incredible he should take the risk even if he can't see the deal. Sometimes the deals you miss teach you the most about balancing your heart and your head.

I'm a serial property buyer, but that doesn't mean I'm a stupid risk taker. Quite the contrary. Of course, like anybody, I get excited about a new investment, whether it's my own or for my MyHouseRE.com clients. But I don't let excitement overwhelm my judgment. As I've said, a lot of making money in real estate is about timing. Too often, people buy just because everyone else is. But if you buy at the top of the market, you're a fool. I tell my clients, be one of the first to discover an area or a new project. How? Here's a checklist I use to determine if an area is about to boom:

1. Is it an older, established area where a developer is coming in and buying property? You can find out about such transactions at the county assessor's office. I bought in a community called Renaissance Commons in Boynton Beach in 2004 because I knew from my research that a company called Compson Associates had just acquired the biggest vacant parcel of land in eastern Palm Beach County, and were planning on building restaurants and retail there. Such development always increases the value of the surrounding residential property. So I bought and in the last year Palm Beach County real estate has appreciated 23 percent.

2. When you learn about redevelopment plans for a neglected downtown or a commercial district. In-fill, mixed-use development (street-level businesses with condos above) is becoming more common in urban areas, and it can increase property values.

3. Look at an aerial view of the land. Is there vacant land around where you're thinking of buying? If there is, that means there's room for population growth. *Population growth is the single most important factor in determining where to buy.* More people means greater demand for places to live. If you go to one of the Las Vegas projects we're selling, South Gate Las Vegas (www.southgatelasvegas.com) and click on Location, you'll see an aerial view. Plenty of empty space still remaining. That means more residential and commercial development and appreciation for your property.

4. Get population growth figures from the chamber of commerce. Growth is good. The population in the three miles surrounding South Gate Las Vegas has grown 70 percent in three years.

5. Find out about employers moving to the area. Are any corporate headquarters or major divisions of a corporation moving to the area? Jobs attract people and that means more homes and more need for businesses.

Using the checklist helps you buy early, before prices go up. If you get excited and you're one of the last people to buy, guess what's happened since the project went up for sale? Demand has driven the price up. That's when your judgment should trump your adrenaline. Walk away. Smart risk divers know when to walk away and when not to.

KENDRA'S RULE OF RISK 13

Sometimes you have to miss out on a big deal to know what it takes to see the next one coming.

START THEM DIVING YOUNG

I honestly believe that risk attitudes are cemented by the time we're kids in our teenage years. Too often, kids learn to fear failure, so they never try anything new. I think it's critically important for parents to instill in their kids when they are very young that risk is desirable (as long as it's smart risk) and that taking risks and failing is okay. Kids should be taught when they take a risk and fall flat to get back up, learn from their mistakes and try again, only smarter this time. Parents should not punish their kids for brave risks, but reward them, win or lose.

As I've said, I was lucky enough to receive this kind of positive reinforcement from my parents. My mother taught me the value of practice in going from being bad at a sport to becoming good. Because I played a lot of sports, my teams often scrimmaged against the guys. I learned that women could do as well as men. If a guy is good in soccer, a girl can be better. Not all children are as lucky as I was. That's why when I speak to kids,

I make sure to tell them that they can do anything. Kids like me because they've seen me on *The Apprentice;* they don't know a thing about my real estate career, nor do they care. But on the show they saw people who were brave, self-confident and creative—exactly as they would like to be. When I talk with kids, I make sure to tell them to chase their dreams.

Kids dream big. They don't know their dreams may be impossible until some adult comes along and thoughtlessly bursts their bubble. Imagine what would happen if we instilled so much self-belief in our kids before they hit the pessimistic adult world that they kept right on dreaming those childhood dreams. Our world could be transformed in a short time by the power of those dreams.

I think as you move ahead into your risk taking, you must keep something of that childlike dreamer in you. Temper it with experience and a good dose of common sense, but keep the sense of wonder and possibility you had when you believed in miracles. After all, Walt Disney ran into obstacle after obstacle when he tried to get Disneyland and later Disney World built, but he clung to his vision—the vision of a man with a great deal of child in him—of the happiest place on earth, and he made it happen. Change is an act of will, but also of faith, the kind of faith you find in the child that's inside you.

KENDRA'S EIGHT RULES FOR RISK DIVING

In this chapter, we're going to talk about what it means to become what I call a "risk diver," a person who approaches risk with the same attitude as a skydiver. The basic principles behind both—get good training, prepare, attend to every detail—are the same, but there are some different principles to smart, successful risk taking in business and in life that bear some explanation.

I've come up with eight rules that every would-be risk diver should follow and every experienced risk diver should continue to practice. Remember, even if you've jumped out of a plane 1,000 times, it only takes one mistake to make jump 1,001 your last. If you learn these rules, live them and master them, together with some of the other lessons I'm going to share in upcoming chapters, you'll be able to leap out of your comfort zone with security as well as euphoria. Onward.

Rule 1: Don't Let Anybody Tell You What Your Risk Is

What's a major risk for you may seem mundane to someone else. Don't let anyone convince you that what for you is a major step out of your comfort zone is actually no big deal. Risk is different for everyone. It's nobody else's business but yours.

For me, buying a rental property is like falling off a log, because I've done it so many times. But for you, signing those first papers for your first income property might seem terrifying. There's nothing wrong with feeling that way, as long as you don't let the fear of risk control you. The key is understanding: if you know your fear is normal, you can acknowledge it, set it aside, and take the action you know is sound and fiscally wise.

There are many ways to risk. Some risks will combine many of these aspects. For instance, if you start a new company in your hometown, you're taking a financial risk (what if the company tanks?), an emotional risk (any business venture is emotional), and a social risk (if your company fails, what happens to your standing in the community?).

The point is, there's no right or wrong risk. There's no risk that's more or less important to take than another. It's personal. It all depends on what's outside your comfort zone and on the chance that your risk can get you closer to your ultimate goal of financial prosperity and personal independence. I know people who think nothing of diving into a deal to buy a $2 million multi-unit residential property but who could never get up in front of a crowd of people and speak. Risk is relative. Start as big or small as you feel comfortable with and work your way up.

Rule 2: The More People Tell You You're Crazy, the More Likely You're on the Right Track.

Ah, conventional wisdom. "They say that . . ." And so on. Who are "they," anyway? There's an aspect of American culture that's hard-wired to maintain the status quo, to keep things going just the way they are. Yet our greatest heroes have often been those people who have deliberately defied conventional wisdom: Ben Franklin, Thomas Edison, Eleanor Roosevelt, Jackie Robinson, and others. There's an inherent pressure in society to conform, to stick to what's already known and to do what's expected. That's understandable—if all you want is what society gives you: the nine-to-five job, the house in the suburbs, two weeks of vacation every year. But what if you want more? You have to defy the cultural pressure. You need to be a maverick. You've got to be willing to be thought of as nuts.

The one thing I love about conventional wisdom is this: it's a wonderful standard against which you can measure your own risks. In my experience, the more unconventional and original a plan is, the more people will tell you, in no uncertain terms, that you're nuts. The farther you stray from the accepted way of doing things, the louder they will become in their objections. This is a great sign. It means you're going against their expectations and not following the crowd. Not following the crowd gives you the best chance of finding an opportunity that no one else has exploited.

EXAMPLE: My parents thought I was crazy when I left the magazine to go into real estate. They wanted me to get a good job where I would have benefits and insurance. They didn't understand why I would want to go into real estate and be my own boss, why I would want to go into something where I wasn't paid and had no sense of structure. But even back then, I knew that when the sky is the limit, you can make nothing or everything. You can be as great as you want. All my friends were getting good jobs with benefits, and I was okay with that lack of security. The harder I worked, the more I made. The harder my friends worked, the more their bosses made.

This isn't to say that you should ignore methods that have proved to work in the past. Anything that works is your friend: don't be a maverick for its own sake. You'll end up doing twice as much work reinventing new ways to do something that someone else has already figured out how to do. The key is to take proven methods and do something original with them. If you want to develop land into a hotel, great. There are time-tested ways for getting through the permitting process and all the rest. But put your own original, unconventional spin on the idea: build an environmentally friendly "eco-resort" in a region where there isn't one. So-called "experts" will scream and rend their garments and prophesy doom. Smile and know you're on the right road.

Now for a caveat. When people tell you you're crazy and headed for ruin, know who's talking. There are two types of Cassandras in this world:

1. **The self-appointed defender of the status quo.** This person doesn't have a concrete reason for opposing what you're doing; she's probably envious that she doesn't have the guts to try it herself.

2. **The reasoned advisor.** This is someone you know well, maybe a mentor or counselor, who has specific reasons why she thinks your venture might be foolish. If this person has credibility, listen carefully and act accordingly.

Rule 3: You Don't "Accident" into a Worthwhile Risk

When you're set on being a risk diver, you've got to keep your eyes, ears, and mind open at all times. You must train yourself to spot a potentially great opportunity—to see opportunity where others only see risk, to put A and B together and see the possibility of C. But while potentially rewarding risks can come into your orbit at any time, seemingly at random, they are usually not random. Most often, they are the result of the people with whom you associate, the reputation you've built for yourself, and the knowledge you've gathered. Just as important, you can't benefit from a risk by accident. Despite what you've heard, a rising tide does not lift all boats. You've got to take conscious action to make a risk pay off, not wait for good things to happen.

What do I mean? Let's look at the first idea, that the risk/reward situations you encounter are rarely random. To be clear, you might run into some tremendous opportunities by chance; it happens all the time. But what's the reward for your risk? As personal branding guru Peter Montoya says, "Hope is not a success strategy."

Ninety percent of the time, risk/reward scenarios that enter your life are going to be the result of specific actions or decisions: being in the right place at the right time, having the education to recognize the significance of a shift in the market, building a network of quality people, acting with integrity toward the people you work with, and so on. If you're the "go to" guy or girl, it's astonishing how often people will call you "out of the blue"—after they've been referred to you by someone else. That's why it's so important to conduct your affairs in a way that *attracts* the type of opportunities you crave. Whether that means attending regular business networking events and rewarding contacts who bring you great deals or keeping yourself healthy and physically fit at all times, putting yourself in a position to take advantage of risk/reward situations is a big part of finding them in the first place.

As for the second idea—that you can't benefit from a risk by accident—it's the difference between being *fatalistic* and *deterministic.* Fatalists believe that everything is predetermined, so all you have to do is wait and good things will happen to you. I'm sorry, but I think that's a crock. Great things didn't happen to Bill Gates because he waited around for them. He forced the action. That's deterministic. When you encounter a risk/reward situation where the reward makes the risk worthwhile, you don't sit around and wait for the stars to align. You don't let other people act and ask you to come along for the ride, or pick up the crumbs from their great deal. You act. You take deliberate steps. You make a decision that you

> **"The credit belongs to the man who is actually in the arena . . . who spends himself in a worthy cause; who knows in the end the triumph of high achievement, and . . . if he fails, at least fails while daring greatly, so that his place shall never be with those cold and timid souls who neither know victory nor defeat."**
>
> **Theodore Roosevelt**
> **April 23, 1910, speech at the Sorbonne, Paris**

will prepare for and accept the risk ahead for the sake of the opportunity it presents. Then you don't look back.

Rule 4: Develop a BS Detector

For every skilled entrepreneur offering you an opportunity to invest in a company that will show solid, steady growth, there are a hundred fly-by-nighters willing to promise you the moon to get you to jump into a badly planned scheme with a snowball's chance in hell of paying off. The question is, can you spot the con artist? Do you have a BS detector?

If you don't have one, develop one fast. In my business, real estate, it's essential. When I'm talking to a potential tenant for one of the buildings I own, I've got to be able to tell whether or not he's lying to me about his reliability. When I consider a condo conversion project to put my clients into, I've got to look at the plans and, using my experience and judgment, decide if the builder can meet his ambitious completion date or if he's just blowing smoke.

If you're new to smart risk taking, it can be tempting to let excitement overwhelm your better judgment when someone comes to you with a risk/reward situation that's too tasty to pass up. That's when you've got to activate your BS detector and become a skeptic. There's nothing wrong with being a skeptic, whether you're dealing with personal relationships or business opportunities. You're simply saying, "Show me." When I'm trying to learn more about a possible opportunity, these are some of the warning signs that will usually bury the needle on my personal BS detector:

— The reward seems to far outweigh the risk. The whole thing seems too good to be true.

— The details of the deal are incomplete.

— There's no transparency. When I ask about details, I hear, "You don't need to know about that."

— Nothing is in writing.

— Someone I trust expresses doubts about the person bringing me the deal.

— The deal appears to contradict common sense, such as a plan to buy expensive real estate at the peak of an overheated market.

When I run into signals like these, I will usually excuse myself and not look back. This opportunity is not for me. The few times I haven't listened to my BS detector, I've regretted it. I always listen to it now.

Over time, you'll develop the perception to know the difference between a person who's asking you to be part of an audacious, daring risk with a real chance of a payoff and a fool or crook trying to get you involved in a pipe dream. It's a crucial skill to have, because the more successful or high-profile you are, the more people will approach you with can't-miss opportunities. Know which ones to miss.

EXAMPLE: You can tell the difference between the people with integrity and the BS slingers by the words they use. If somebody hits me with terms like "Great deal," "You can't lose," "You'll make so much," and "Everybody's doing it," I walk away. Those are vague terms used to appeal to emotion or greed. Beware of people who provide no facts. I listen to people who give me facts: population growth in an area is 1 percent higher than citywide average, corporations are opening headquarters, and so on. When someone provides data and not a sales pitch, then the deal is worth investigating. Remember, you shouldn't have to be "sold" on a good risk. It should be obvious to you.

Rule 5: Risk Decreases as You Develop a System That Anticipates and Prepares for It

Risk is unpredictable, but it's not impossible to measure. You can almost graph it on a chart like this:

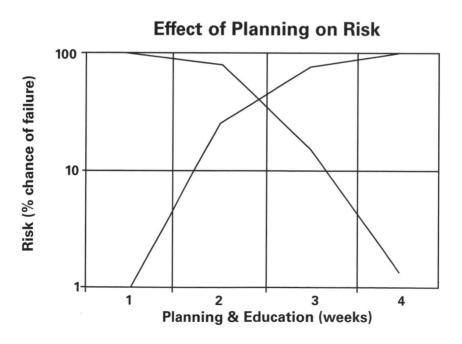

Effect of Planning on Risk

Notice that the more you plan and learn, the lower your risk level. There's a direct relationship between planning and anticipation and the risk of failure. But that's not enough for habitual risk takers, the entrepreneurial types (like me) who enjoy pursuing new opportunities and reaping the rewards. We rely on a system that prepares us to handle any risks that might come along. That's what I suggest you do. A risk management system leaves nothing to chance, and when you're putting hard-earned dollars, months of your time, or your reputation on the line, you don't want too many surprises.

These are some of the key components of a strong risk management system:

— A research team that can immediately begin checking the bona fides of the people or businesses you're considering getting involved with. This can mean anything from searching the Internet to checking the local newspaper archives for stories good and bad. You shouldn't have to pay for the research sources; they should be widely available. I'd suggest contracting with a group of graduate students for conducting the actual searches, because they know research methodology and always need the money.

— A network of contacts who can tell you about the people involved in the deal.

— At least one source of capital with whom you have a long-standing, trusting relationship. This can be an individual "hard money" lender or an institution you've worked with before.

— A Power Team of vendors who can provide valuable services on short notice, such as graphic designers, web developers, contractors, or printers.

— A savvy attorney on retainer.

— A computer backup system where you archive all e-mails, documents, etc.

Your system will vary depending on your business, your personal preferences, and what types of risk you're facing. For example, if you're in the political arena, you can't live without a great publicist. For my My HouseRE.com clients, I employ a risk management system with several parts:

— Demographic research on the area. If you know what drives the market, you're more in control of the deal.

— Knowing the age of the property, an effective predictor of possible problems.

— I try to point people in the right direction to rent their units, such as lease options or signing up with corporate relocation companies. I have them prospect at the local gym, because I've found that people who care about their health and pay a monthly gym fee would probably make good tenants.

— I disclose all risk factors before my clients get into a deal. I show them ways to negate some risks and help them understand which ones are out of their control. It's important to me not to backtrack with my clients, not to overpromise to them.

Having a risk management system you can put into action as soon as an opportunity crosses your path can help you spot problems at a distance, identify alternatives to the deal you've been presented, and find people to know or to avoid.

Rule 6: Defy the Trend

Copying what somebody else is doing is a basic human impulse; it seems to reduce the risk of failure if we just fall in line behind the other guy. But while that's wise if you're on a narrow mountain trail, it's very foolish if you're trying to chart your own course as an investor or entrepreneur. Defy the trend by finding out what the other guy is doing wrong and taking a different tack. Or take his idea and do it better; multibillion-dollar businesses have been built by improving on someone else's idea. Just ask Apple Computer, which saw their graphical user interface turned into the world-dominating Windows by Microsoft.

There are several reasons to avoid copying someone else outright. First of all, by the time a trend is reported as such, it's often played out. Another reason is that if someone's already taking advantage of a trend, the cost of your doing the same thing will have increased. That's why I bring my investors to new real estate projects early, often while they're still under construction. They get in early and set the price, rather than coming in late when the price is established and they have no leverage.

But the most important reason to defy trends is simple: if someone's done it before, it has less value than something new and innovative. Going against the grain gives you what marketers call "first mover advantage": you're the first one in your market to bring a business idea to the customer. There's no competition, whereas when you're just the latest player in a saturated market, you're competing with a lot of people, all of whom had a head start on you.

Let's say your big dream—and big risk—is to open your own high-end gourmet restaurant. You live in a city where there are already half a dozen elegant "be seen at" Italian bistros, so why would you open another? The others are entrenched, with a loyal clientele. You'd only be seen as a copycat. Even if your food were better, you'd be fighting an uphill battle against dug-in opponents.

But let's say you look around your city and make a strategic decision. You see not a single Cuban restaurant in town, yet you know there's a substantial Caribbean population in the region. So you open a stylish Cuban cafe with live music and a luxurious cigar room. You're something new, something no one else is doing. You have no competition. You can set the pace and capture the loyal lovers of Cuban food and culture before anyone else even makes a move. And you did it by going against the trend.

Like everything else I'm suggesting, defying the trend isn't an absolute. It's important to make sure that you're not going against the grain for no reason. Some trend-defying ideas haven't been pursued for a reason. Opening a pork barbecue restaurant in an Orthodox Jewish or Muslim neighborhood? Probably not a sound business idea. Take a careful look at the trends you're dealing with as you approach your opportunity. Has the trend played itself out? Is it at its peak with nowhere to go but down? Are there people who have exploited it but badly, so that there's room for you to jump in and do it right? Look at Starbucks. Coffeehouses had been around for centuries, but they took an old idea, gave it their own spin, and built a multibillion-dollar global brand.

> **"The tragedy of life doesn't lie in not reaching your goal. The tragedy lies in having no goal to reach."**
>
> **Benjamin E Mays, former President, Morehouse College, in a commencement address at Barnard College, *New York Times*, 1985**

Rule 7: Don't Manufacture Unnecessary Risk

People who violate this rule drive me crazy. They cross the line from smart risk taking into thrill seeking. This is the equivalent of jumping out of a plane, cutting your parachute loose, and trying to glide down to a fellow jumper so you can hang on to him and get down in tandem. The risks are staggering, the payoff no greater. Still, a great many people, from entrepreneurs to athletes, manufacture risks all the time.

What does it mean to "manufacture risk"? It means that to the risks already inherent in a real estate deal, a new business, an Everest climb, or a marriage proposal, you go out of your way to add new risks that weren't there and aren't necessary. That might mean something like:

— Starting your business in an office that's twice the lease price of the one across the street.

— If you're buying an old house to rehabilitate and flip, waiving the inspection because you want to close the deal faster. What if the foundation is bad?

— On a mountain climb where people normally use bottled oxygen, choosing to climb without oxygen because you think it's macho.

— Doubling your investment in an unproven startup company before it's even opened its doors.

Manufacturing risk means taking action that increases your risk of failure without correspondingly increasing the reward. You're throwing additional obstacles in your path out of ego, ignorance, or misplaced enthusiasm. This often happens when an experienced risk taker becomes too convinced of his or her own ability to deal with any surprise. These folks might add an extra risk factor in order to make things more "interesting."

To me, extra risks aren't interesting. Interesting is a high-stakes deal where I've planned for the visible risks as best I can, with a satisfying payoff for everybody at the end. I don't need to walk the high wire to get my kicks. Especially when you're beginning to step out of that comfort zone, do everything you can to reduce your risk factors. Take it from me, there are enough twists, turns, and gremlins built into any risky situation without deliberately adding more.

Rule 8: Control What You Can and Don't Worry About the Rest—Pull the Ripcord and Hope for the Best

Finally, after you've done your due diligence, talked to people in the know, conducted your research, made your plans, and taken all the steps humanly possible to bring down your risk exposure, it's time to go for it. You can't control every risk factor or predict every unexpected event. Sometimes trouble is a hurricane; you usually have warning and time to carry your valuables out of harm's way. Sometimes it's a tornado, hitting without warning so that all you can do is hang on and try to survive. Which kind of trouble you'll run into isn't for you to decide.

All you can do is control what you can and prepare for what you can't, then go for it and dive in. Do it. Don't hesitate. I've seen too many would-be moguls who found the deals, did the prep, and got their pieces in place, then couldn't pull the trigger. I suspect it was because they liked the feeling of preparing to manage risk, but then didn't have what it takes to jump out of that comfort zone. It's a shame, but they'll probably never achieve the kind of success that true risk takers will.

Remember my story about Charles passing on the farmland that eventually became the multimillion-dollar Mall at Wellington Green, the most luxurious commercial center in Palm Beach County? That's what I'm talking about. Charles had the deal in front of him but doubted his vision. He won't make that mistake again; that deal would have made him a millionaire many times over.

Some things are a matter of luck. Others are for the gods to decide, or karma if your beliefs swing that way. There's a famous saying from Sherlock Holmes that goes, "Once you eliminate everything else, what remains, no matter how unlikely, must be the truth." My take on that is, "Once you have done everything you can do, there's nothing more that can be done." Don't overprepare. If you do, you'll become an obsessive planner and not a risk taker. That's fine if you want to be part of someone else's support team, but not if you want to lead. When you're confident in your opportunity and in your planning, that's the time to keep your eyes on your goal, draw a deep breath, and jump.

7.

TEN STEPS FOR TURNING RISK INTO OPPORTUNITY

"A man who sees the possibility opening before him and does not try to grasp it, even at the risk of destroying himself and his country, is either a saint or a mediocrity."

SIMONE WEIL, FRENCH PHILOSOPHER AND MYSTIC

"If you think you are too small to have an impact, try going to bed with a mosquito." That's one of my favorite quotes, and it's from a woman named Anita Roddick. Never heard of her? You have, even if you don't realize it. Anita is a restless Englishwoman who, in her twenties, loved to travel and experience other cultures. But she wanted to do more than run the small hotel she and her husband owned. She wanted to make a difference. She saw exploitative labor practices around the world and she wanted to start a business that would buy fair trade products and sell quality, healthy cosmetics at a fair price. She and her husband sold the hotel, invested everything they had, and opened their first business next to a funeral home in the English seaside resort town of Brighton. And every day, they thought about only one thing: surviving until the next day.

Think you know who Anita Roddick is now? If you said she's the founder and public face of the Body Shop, give yourself a gold star. Today, the company built on the mantra "profits with principles" has more than 1,400 locations in nearly 50 countries. And all because Anita followed her passion and took the risk that people would buy natural, environmentally friendly cosmetics, even when no one else was selling them.

Anita Roddick is a textbook example of someone who followed the first and most important of my Ten Steps for Turning Risk into Opportunity: Know What You Want. I'm always surprised when I talk to people who, when I ask them what they want in life, say, "To be rich." Wealth is a state of being, not a goal. You don't create wealth or change the world by saying, "I want to get wealthy" or "I want to stop children from being exploited in the Third World." Instead, you've got to be able to say, "I want to launch a software company and take it public in five years" or "I want to design a cheap way for rural areas to generate electricity." Anita Roddick wanted to start a business that would prosper while establishing the market for responsibly made, environmentally respectful beauty products. She didn't get there by accident. She knew what she wanted and went after it.

HOW FAR ARE YOU TRYING TO LEAP?

We've been talking a lot about different kinds of risk and how to jump into risk boldly but intelligently. Now it's time to get down to business and look at the ten specific steps you've got to follow to take a risky situation and turn it into opportunity. As you've no doubt figured out by now, reaching any goal involves risk. But the more different your goal is from your current life, the greater the risk.

If you're a medical billing professional and your goal is to start your own medical billing company, there's risk but it's reduced. After all, you have the knowledge, the contacts, and the technology. But if you're a college dropout hanging drywall for $10 an hour and your dream is to open your own four-star gourmet restaurant in Manhattan, you're going to have to take a much greater risk to make that happen. The farther you want to go from where you are, the longer and more dangerous the leap you've got to make.

KENDRA'S RULE OF RISK 14

The farther the goal, the longer the jump.

But no matter how long your leap, it doesn't have to be reckless and destined for disaster. That's where the Ten Steps come in. Being systematic is your best defense against the inherent danger in risk, whether it's financial, emotional, political, or any other kind. By applying the steps to every risk you encounter and taking each step in succession, you'll not only be more prepared for everything that comes your way, you'll be better able to adjust, think on your feet, and make the moves you need to see the gold at the end of the rainbow.

Ready?

STEP 1: DECIDE WHAT YOU WANT

You can't do anything until you know what you want. This goes back to Risk Diving Rule 3: *You don't "accident" into a worthwhile risk.* It's very unlikely that what you want—and the risks and opportunities that go along with it—are going to drop into your lap. You're going to have to make them happen. And that begins with deciding what you want.

Make your want specific; you're plotting out a strategy to handle risk and reach your goals, but you won't reach them if they're vague. Want to be wealthy? Of course you do—who doesn't? But *how* are you going to get wealthy? Are you going to become a real estate investor? Start your own company? Write a bestselling book? Beat the craps tables in Vegas? How's it going to happen? These are the kinds of questions you should be asking yourself.

There's another factor to consider when you're deciding what you want: what turns you on? What are you passionate about? As I said before, I love buying residential properties. It's a turn-on for me. Every day that I'm in the process of closing a deal for another property, I wake up excited. It's important that you choose a "want" that fires your passions the same way. As personal development guru Denis Waitley says, "Chase your passion, not your pension." If you pursue the goal of wealth but in the process spend twenty years doing something you hate, guess what? You won't get wealthy. Because you're not a robot. You'll sabotage yourself by doing a poor job. Turning risk into success takes enormous energy and commitment, and you can't have that if you don't love what you're doing. So ask yourself: "What do I love, and how can I get rich doing it?"

One more twist to this step: think long term. There's another name for short-term wealth and success programs: scams. They don't exist, unless you're a psychic who picks winning lottery numbers. The "want" you choose should set you toward reaching your goal in the long term, not in a matter of months. I'm not saying that you need to toil for twenty-five years to build a million-dollar net worth, but that setting your sights on reaching your goal in three or five years is not unreasonable.

These are some good examples of "wants." Note that below the general want is the specific goal:

General: Be a millionaire by age thirty.
Specific: Buy and flip my first home in twelve months.

General: Own my own business.
Specific: Use my experience to start my own financial planning practice.

General: Become a successful screenwriter.
Specific: Complete feature film script within the next six months.

Step 1 is about looking at the map of your life and figuring out where you want to go. And when you're doing that, you don't just point a finger and say, "I'm going to New York." You choose a city, a precise destination. If you take a few side roads along the way, so what? You always know where you're going. Once you do, it's time for Step 2.

STEP 2: FIGURE OUT WHAT YOU MUST DO TO GET IT

Are you a list maker? I am. As busy as my schedule is, if I didn't have to-do lists to keep me organized, I would lose my mind.

KENDRA'S RULE OF RISK 15

Risk takers are list makers.

That's hard for some people to swallow. List making is seen as anal retentive and fussy, while risk taking is supposed to be wild and impulsive. But as we've learned, good risks are smart, planned-for risks, and that means making lists.

Once you know what you want, it's time to sit down and write down all the actions you'll need to take to get what you want. Some will be risky; others won't be. But all are necessary; you can't get from here to there without them. I'm not just talking about the glamorous things, either. You need to write down even the grunt work, from the classes you need to take to the house you'll need to rent if you decide to chuck it all and move to Hollywood. Spend some time, do some research, and if it takes a week to finish your list, so be it.

What does such a list look like? It's pretty simple. Let's say you decided that you want to get rich buying and flipping homes—that is, buying properties in need of work, rehabilitating them quickly, and reselling them for a fast profit. But you don't know much about real estate. Make a list with three columns. In the first column, list the specific actions you need to take to get what you want. Your chronological list might look like this:

— Rent office space.

— Buy books about flipping properties.

— Attend a highly rated seminar or boot camp.

— Talk to real estate investors in my area.

— Join my local Real Estate Investors Association chapter.

— Print business cards.

— Talk to lenders and title companies.

— Drive around my area looking for likely homes.

— Get a dedicated "deal" cell phone.

— And, finally, quit my job.

That's just a partial list, but you get the picture. Visualize all the things you'll need to get what you want, then walk yourself through every step, focusing not only on the big picture but the small details, like business cards, phones, and so on. Use your second column to write down how you'll achieve each of the items on your list—sources of classes, organization contact information, names of people you know and such.

With your list done, it's time for Step 3.

STEP 3: IDENTIFY THE RISKS INVOLVED

Not all the items on your to-do list will be risky. Some will be totally mundane. But some will represent real risks with real dangers. At this stage, you've got to figure out what those risks are and what's at stake.

Look at your list and in the third column, start writing down all the risks associated with each of the actions. Stick to major risks involving substantial amounts of money or time. You don't care about the risk of having your business cards printed badly. You just order another batch. Here, you're concerned with risks that could get you sued, ruin you financially, waste months or years of your time, wreck important relationships, or even damage your health. Using the same example of someone trying to start a career buying and flipping houses, let's look at a list of actions and their likely risks:

ACTION	RISKS
Rent office space.	Taking on extra expense I can't afford
Buy books about flipping properties.	Waste time reading books that can't help me
Attend a highly rated seminar or boot camp.	Paying hundreds of dollars for information I can't use Wasting days of my time Travel expenses
Talk to real estate investors in my area.	Wasting time Being targeted by con artists
Join my local Real Estate Investors Association chapter.	None
Print business cards.	Expense of design and printing
Talk to lenders and title companies.	Investing time with companies that may not be able to help me
Drive around my area looking for likely homes.	Gasoline Getting into a dangerous neighborhood
Get a dedicated "deal" cell phone.	An additional monthly expense
Quit my job.	Running out of money Being evicted Losing health insurance Going bankrupt

Create a catalog of possible risks associated with your goal, but don't let that list discourage you. The idea here isn't to dwell on the negative, but to look realistically at the risks involved in going after what you want, so you can proceed with both eyes open. This is also the step where you should ask yourself, "Is this too much risk for me?" If you're uncomfortable with the risks in front of you, back off, rethink your plan, and start again. Remember, it's wise, not cowardly, to have second thoughts about a risk that you might not be ready to handle.

Once you know the risks you could face (and are ready to face them), you can take on Step 4.

STEP 4: FIGURE OUT HOW TO MINIMIZE YOUR RISK FACTORS

This is simply one of the most important skills all successful people possess. I find that really successful individuals—captains of industry, real estate moguls, entrepreneurs, award-winning artists—approach risk in one of two ways: either they plan obsessively how to deal with it or they jump in with both feet and trust to their instincts and talents to bail them out. More often than not, it's the planners who come out ahead.

There are many strategies for minimizing risk; here are those that I've found most effective:

— **EDUCATION.** This is the best of them all. The more you know, the less likely you are to make a costly mistake. No matter what your goal, find out if there are re-

> "Those who misrepresent the normal experiences of life, who decry being controversial, who shun risk, are the enemies of the American way of life, whatever the piety of their vocal professions and the patriotic flavor of their platitudes."
>
> Henry M. Wriston, President Emeritus, Brown University, *Wall Street Journal*, 1960

sources you can use to educate yourself in your area of interest. This could mean anything from taking classes at a local university, to attending an intensive weekend real estate seminar, to picking up an outstanding set of books and audio CDs that you listen to in your spare time. Whether you're looking to move into owning a nightclub or becoming a day trader, information is your most valuable weapon. Pay attention to things like historical trends and legal issues. Knowing the history of an industry, a city, or a person can help you predict what will happen in the future, while knowing legal matters can save your behind when the time comes for negotiations and contracts. Resources like the Learning Annex can be a great help in this area, providing courses on everything from starting a small business to getting government funding.

— **FORESIGHT.** I like to practice what I call "anticipatory thinking." That is, before I jump into a risky endeavor, I like to look ahead at all the possible obstacles and situations that might appear in my path and figure out how to deal with them or even turn them to my advantage. This proactive approach to risk means I'm more prepared than most other people for what comes along. Developing foresight doesn't require a crystal ball, tarot cards, or any other special equipment. Just sit down and clear your mind of the immediate tasks you have in front of you. Look down the road ahead of you—a week, a month, three months—as you pursue this risky opportunity. Based on what you know about the people, money, or businesses involved, what likely obstacles or unexpected opportunities can you see popping up in your path? Is a partner likely to back out? Who, and how will you handle it? Is there a fifty-fifty chance a source of funding will dry up or that hurricane season (an annual threat here in Florida) will impact your plans? If so, what contingency plans should you have in place to keep things going? Foresight isn't magical. It's developed by taking the time to think about things that might happen and to prepare for them. If they don't happen, great. If they do, you're ready and you'll stay on course where others fail.

One of the best examples I've seen of foresight is a real estate investor here in South Florida. This guy saw years ago that in the Florida Keys, a major boating area, limits on development were going to create a serious shortage of boat slips in the coming years. So this investor starting buying boat slips. While his colleagues were buying residential properties, he was buying boat slips. While they told him he was nuts, he was quietly acquiring whole marinas. Guess what? Development boomed and so did demand for boating facilities. This gentleman had cornered the market on boat slips and marina space, and he's been cleaning up for years because he owns the lion's share of a rare commodity. All because he had the foresight to predict the direction the market was likely to take. A gamble, but boy, did it pay off!

— **PREPARATION.** Have all your ducks in their proverbial rows before you jump into your risky situation. If you're leaving your job, have six months' worth of expense money saved in a money market account. Have your cell phone programmed with numbers you need, your loans lined up and approved, your research done and copious notes entered into your Palm Pilot for easy referral, your Power Team selected and brought up to speed on what you're doing, a schedule mapped out down to the day, and your best business suits cleaned and pressed. Details matter. Take care of all the small things before the days get busy and crazy, because they will. You'll spend less time scrambling and more time taking meaningful action.

— **DOCUMENTATION.** Get everything in writing, and keep records of *everything*. In a world where people can and will stab you in the back, written records are your safety net. Take notes of meetings and phone conversations, then enter them into a word processing program so they're dated (better yet, have your secretary do it). Keep every e-mail, fax, and, of course, contract. If newspaper articles come out that relate to your project, clip and save. Record important conversations (with the other party's permission). File everything by date so you can access it more easily later on. That way, in case of a lawsuit or something as common as a misunderstanding about what was said, you'll have a paper trail to back up your side of the story.

— **RELATIONSHIPS.** Of course, if you choose the people you work with wisely, you won't have to worry about being stabbed in the back, because you'll be watching out for each other. In any kind of business, no decision is more important than selecting those with whom you work. I like to rely on Warren Buffett's three questions when deciding whether or not to work with someone: "Do I like this person?" "Do I respect this person?" "Do I trust this person?" If I can't answer "Yes" to all three, I won't work with that person. You'll notice that there's nothing about skill sets or professional experience in those criteria. Those are important (in a real estate deal, an exceptionally trustworthy, respectable, and likeable golf cart salesman isn't going to help you much), but they're not deal breakers.

I'd rather have a partner of moderate skill and great character than a partner with thirty years' experience who I can't trust. The partner with character is going to do the work necessary to be an asset to me and he's not going to screw me when my back is turned. If you choose good people and take care of them, they will take care of you. That's one of the most important lessons you can learn in minimizing risk.

— **DIVERSIFICATION.** Just as in investing, the more you spread your risk around, the more you reduce it. My investments are all in real estate, but they're in rentals and condo conversions; in detached homes, attached homes, and apartments; and in areas all over South Florida. Real estate teaches you about an area. I invest in different areas and watch how the markets react.

I'll never put all my eggs in one basket; I'll always have multiple deals working at any time. If some fall through, others are sure to hit big. Then I can take the lessons I learned from the failures and apply them someplace else. Now, if you're jumping into something as huge as starting your own business, you're not going to be able to start another one on the side "just in case." That's ridiculous. But you can diversify by taking other, less risky actions that can be your cushion in case things don't work out. For instance, if you own a piece of property, maybe that's the time to sell it and cash out, so that if you need to pump emergency cash into your new restaurant, you've got it. Sure, you're risking not getting top dollar. But one risk feeds the other; you reduce the odds of your bigger risk (your startup business failing) by taking a smaller risk (selling your lake cabin).

— **TIMING.** Life is timing! I can't tell you how many great opportunities I've found and how many sure things haven't worked out because of timing. Stockbrokers will tell you that only fools try to time the market. That's true. But you can time your risks. Look at the environment surrounding that risk. Let's say your risk is that you want to quit your job and go back to school full time to get your law degree. Before you do, step back and ask some questions about the timing of your decision. Can you pay for law school? Is the job market for lawyers in your geographic area likely to be strong in three years? Will your current lifestyle accommodate years of study and exams? If not, can you handle three years of changes necessary to accomplish your goal? Are there likely to be opportunities soon after law school (investments, for example) that you will be unable to capitalize on because of massive student loan debt? Basically, is the timing of your risk right, based on what you know and what you can speculate about with accuracy? In real estate, the questions are always about the value of a property, the status of the area, and the general direction of the market. Pay attention to timing. If the timing isn't right for you, wait—but get ready for when the timing *is* right.

EXAMPLE: I have clients who buy into properties and I remind them that real estate is a long-term commitment if you want to build wealth. People might buy a project and establish $50,000 equity on a $200,000 purchase in a short time, then they want to cash in their equity. But if they studied the area, they'd learn that in three years a huge mixed-use property will be built three blocks away. South Gate Las Vegas is right next to South Coast casino in Las Vegas. It will take five years for the south end of the Las Vegas Strip to merge with the South Strip, and I know there will be people who will become impatient and sell their properties in a year, and they will do well. But the people who can wait the five years will eventually own a piece of the Strip and see substantial returns beyond anything we can a anticipate now. We get excited when we're on the fringe of big returns, and we sell when we should do research and learn about the regional market (the three- to five-mile radius around the property). The market will dictate how long you should hold any property.

— **COMMON SENSE.** This is a surprisingly elusive quality in business, and that's why you see so many would-be millionaires still toiling in nine-to-five jobs twenty years after they were sure they were going to hit it big. Listen to your common sense. If something looks too good to be true, it is. If a potential partner has been kicked out of half a dozen other deals, there's a reason. If a price is too low, it's not because the seller is feeling generous. If you feel like you're in over your head, you probably need to bring someone with more experience into your deal and cut them a share as well. Don't get greedy. Create win-win situations for everybody. None of this is brain surgery, but it's amazing how often commonsense wisdom is ignored by people who only have their eyes on the prize. Keep your eyes on the prize, but keep your ear to the ground and your nose sniffing for danger and opportunity at all times.

EXAMPLE: Sometimes you've just got to do the obvious. In 2003, I bought a townhouse on the Intracoastal Waterway where the entire eastern side of the community was open to the water. It's premium property, very desirable. I had a client in my office who bought in the same community, but he was worried about the market peaking even though waterfront property almost always appreciates, because they're not making more waterfront. The guy sold after a year and made $110,000, a nice profit. But two years later, he's kicking himself because the unit I bought for $190,000 is worth $380,000 now, and it's going to keep increasing in value.

STEP 5: MITIGATE

Remember when we talked about the "Three Ates" back in chapter 1? Mitigation means finding all the possible ways you can benefit from taking a risk, even if the main opportunity falls through. For instance, you plan to get in on the ground floor of a hot commercial development, spend months working on the deal, and then at the last minute it's killed by the city because toxic contamination is discovered at the building site. But because you worked on cultivating relationships with the developers, lenders, and your would-be partners, you walk away with a Rolodex full of great contacts and several other possible deals already in the works. While you might feel you wasted your time, the contacts could prove to be very profitable in the future. That's mitigation.

Look at your risk and write down all the possible ways you could benefit from jumping in even if things don't work out. These can include making great contacts for your network, learning new skills, finding other deals, or getting your finances in better shape. Then figure out what you need to do to realize all those benefits as your risk is playing itself out. Even if things don't fall into place this time, you'll be in better shape than when you started, ready to try again.

STEP 6: MAKE YOUR RISK PLAN

Now is the time to draw out your risk plan, your blueprint for turning risk into reward. I suggest making a chart with your primary goal at the top. Below that, list each of the subgoals related to that main goal, such as "closing financing" or "finding an advertising agency." Then for each subgoal, list all the components of achieving that goal:

RISK PLAN WORKSHEET

1. People and contact information	John Smith, (800) 555-1212
2. Cost and source of money	Cost: $275,990
	Interest rate: 5.75, 15-year fixed
	Lender: First Financial, Bob Jones, (888) 345-6789
3. Purchases needed	Carpeting
	Lighting system
4. Services to contract	Carpet layers, Ace Carpets (877) 987-6543
	Painters, Tom Adams, 333-4455
5. Important deadlines	Documents submitted: August 10
	Closing: August 15
	Tenant move-in: October 1
6. Required information/education	Population growth figures since 2003
	Redevelopment plans for vacant shopping center
7. Details	Check zoning laws with city
	Talk to developer about Internet access

Add any other categories you feel you need. Then for each component, make your to-do list. List everything you must do to reach each subgoal, from conducting research at the county records office to finding an insurance company. Pay special attention to the "Details" column. That's where you'll list everything from sending thank you cards to vendors who help you out to setting up phone service for a new office. Taking care of the small details adds up to either a big load off your mind or a big waste of your time, depending on how you handle them.

By the time you're finished with your risk plan, you'll have an exhaustively detailed road map of your entire risk/reward situation, including the people you're working with, the time frames in which everything has to be accomplished, and the small steps that add up to the big payoff. Leave nothing to chance. There are enough surprises waiting for you in any situation. Don't unnecessarily create more.

Depending on the level of risk you're taking on, you can add one more area to your road map: "Backups." That's where you'll write down your backup resources in case something goes dreadfully awry. If an investor backs out at the last minute, who do you call? If you have a backup listed, you're already on the phone. Not everybody puts backups in their risk plan; that's a decision you'll have to make on a case-by-case basis. But the greater the risk, the more comfortable you'll feel having that second parachute on your back.

> **"Power is given only to those who dare to lower themselves and pick it up. Only one thing matters, one thing; to be able to dare!"**
>
> **Fyodor Dostoyevsky,**
> *Crime and Punishment*

STEP 7: TAKE FAST, DECISIVE ACTION

At this stage, risk is like driving a car in the Indy 500. You've spent weeks tuning, tinkering, and preparing so that everything is in top condition. Why? Because if it's not, you could die. When you finally get to the starting line and your engine is revving, prep time is over. It's time for speed. Time to make aggressive moves, take no prisoners, and act with quickness and precision. You're still not going to take stupid risks, but you're not going to sit back and wait anymore, either.

You've thought, you've made lists, you've mitigated and planned until your fingers were sore. Now's the time for action. When the pieces are all in place and your plan is ready, act and act fast. Most people are not decisive; they'll hem and haw and look for validation from others. They're easy prey for someone like you. You're going to act wisely but decisively. Because you've done your homework and you have your financial house in order, you're going to call and make a firm offer on that rental house while six other buyers are still trying to decide if they want it or not. You'll buy it from under their noses before they even know you were in the game. As the saying goes, "You can't steal in slow motion."

This is the time to get your team moving, each person with his or her role. It's the time to make the phone calls, set up the meetings, and put the ball in the other guy's court. Here's a tip: people love to work with decisive people. Whether you're dealing with bankers, investors, or lawyers, everybody likes working with someone who's done their homework, knows what they want, and doesn't waste anybody's time. You're always looking for an edge, and being someone who others like to work with can give you that edge.

Most important, if you have competitors for the same opportunity (other buyers for an income property or people starting a competing small business, for example), acting quickly and decisively means you set the rules. Now they've got to react to what you've done. And as anyone in any business will tell you, reacting instead of acting gets you in trouble. Once you take the initiative, you can either sit back and watch what the other guy does, prepared to counter, or keep moving and always stay two steps ahead. Either way, it's a huge advantage. You set the price for the property. You're first to market with a new product. You set the legal precedent.

Of course, as soon as you act, the unexpected will appear. That's where Step 8 comes in.

EXAMPLE: Charles closed a deal late in 2005 that's a perfect example of the value of fast action. A woman in our area purchased several estate homes from the developer of a gorgeous waterfront community for $1 million each, but she couldn't execute on one of the sales, so the contract was nonsignable and the developers were faced with the task of putting the home back on the market after they thought they had a deal. Charles found out about the broken deal, contacted the developers the same day, and told them he could turn their nonsignable contract into a signable one and could close in less than two weeks. They jumped at the chance, of course. That's the value of creating a win-win. So Charles bought a waterfront home for $830,000; the next day the developers were asking $1.15 million for an identical home. That's $285,000 in equity overnight. Good thing he didn't hesitate!

As long as Charles holds onto that property, that's paper profit. However, he can leverage that equity by taking out an equity line worth up to 80 percent of that $285,000 and using that money to buy yet another investment property. Owning property in an appreciating market gives you the most precious commodity in investing: flexibility. You can hold property and tap the equity to buy more, or you can take the profit and cash out. You have the choice. We'll talk about exactly how to do this in chapter 9.

STEP 8: THINK ON YOUR FEET
AND DEAL WITH SURPRISES

One thing you'll learn as you venture into more risky situations (and I can tell you from personal experience that there's no way to learn this but to do it) is that no matter how much you anticipate and plan, there are factors in any risk you cannot control. There's an old Army saying that goes, "No battle plan ever survives first contact with the enemy." That means you can plan from now until doomsday, but real life seldom cooperates with plans.

You're skydiving and your main chute doesn't open. That's why you have a reserve chute. That's planning. But a gust suddenly blows you off course and away from the landing zone. That's unexpected circumstance. You've got to think fast and adjust. If you've done your homework and know the local topography, you can steer to a flat space and land safely anyway. You might have to hitchhike back to the drop zone and endure a lot of kidding, but at least you'll be in one piece.

One of the most important lessons I've learned in my years as a risk diver is *never get complacent.* Never assume everything is in the bag until the contracts are signed and the check clears. If you get complacent, you'll get sloppy. You'll let some details slide and find out that your pocket was picked. I find it's always safer to assume things can and will go wrong until they prove otherwise. Then, when a nasty surprise rears up, I don't get angry or frustrated. I just say, "Aha, there you are," and go about taking care of it.

My personal disaster contingency plan consists of multiple untapped home equity lines worth tens of thousands of dollars. That's one of the ways I've turned my real estate investments into cash: once one of my properties appreciates, I go to my lender and open a credit line against the equity in that property. Because this market is appreciating, I've built up substantial equity in my properties, and I have established equity lines that I haven't tapped on several of those properties. The money is available, like a loaded gun, in case a deal comes out of nowhere or I need substantial cash fast in an emergency. Doing this means developing a level of comfort with debt. Debt is not something to fear; it's a tool you can use to create wealth. As long as I don't tap an equity line, I don't pay anything on it. It's not costing me a dime, but it's ready money I can use to pounce on a great deal or to bail myself out in an emergency, such as repairing hurricane damage to one of my rental units. That's one of the ways veteran investors leverage real estate and turn it into cash.

One of the greatest benefits to all this elaborate planning and list making is that you're so organized that when an abrupt reverse of fortune does come along, from legal troubles to a property that fails inspection, you've got the time and brainpower to think on your feet and handle it. When you're stressed, new problems feel like they weigh a million pounds; when things are running like a well-oiled engine, you handle surprises with a couple of phone calls. You stay cool, and thus you're able to overcome sudden obstacles more easily.

Thinking on your feet is a matter of practice. As you involve yourself in more risks and step outside your comfort zone more often, you'll develop the ability to find fast, creative ways to solve problems. That's what I call "thinking around corners." But I find there are two ways to become better at this, too, without just relying on firsthand experience. First, the more you know about the people and businesses in your area, the better. If you need a product or service in an emergency, you'll know who to call. Second, practice anticipatory thinking and ask yourself, "If X happened on a Sunday morning, how would I act to keep my deal from falling through?" Rehearsing how you'll handle unpleasant surprises can help you develop the mindset to become a creative problem solver.

Now, if everything goes reasonably according to plan and your surprises don't sink your opportunity, you'll be thrilled to move on to Step 9.

EXAMPLE: Sometimes contingency planning saves the day. Every deal has its complications and challenges, so you always have to be solution driven. The multisuccessful person sees problems as everyday challenges. In this case, a client was buying an investment property, and with most financing you need six months' reserve cash plus your down payment—that's the law. The developer saw that the buyers had $56,000 in the bank, but knew they might have made large deposits for their down payments and closing costs, so there was no way to know how much they really had in reserve. Now, traditional lenders might throw up a red flag and deny funding. We stepped in with United Mutual Lending, one of our companies, did a verification of deposit using one form, and got the deal done. Finding solutions is an attitude; you have to decide before you start business that day that whatever comes up, you'll find a way to make it work.

STEP 9: REAP THE REWARDS

Congratulations! Your deal is done and you survived. Make sure all the "t's" are crossed and the "i's" dotted, the check's in the bank, and the contracts are signed, then sit back and enjoy the fruits of your labor. It's vital to really savor your successful risks, because taking each one is a big deal. They're affirmations of your abilities and your judgment. Coming through a risk to the reward should be a time of joy, relief, and excitement. Reward yourself with the leisure to enjoy it. Take a vacation. Treat yourself to a fancy night out. Sleep all day. Whatever turns you on.

Reaping the rewards of your risk goes beyond cashing the check or launching your business. It's also vital to take care of people who took care of you. Were there vendors, service providers, or individuals without whom your venture might have failed? Send them a $100 bottle of wine or a $500 check. Thank them and let them know you'll be working with them again. Each time you step outside your comfort zone into a new venture, one of the smartest things you can do is to expand your roster of smart, dependable, honorable people whom you can trust in a pinch. Those are the kinds of people who will help make you rich.

STEP 10: REPEAT!

Now that you've turned one risky situation into an opportunity and a reward, do it again. Step back up to the plate and take another swing. You're going to find that exiting your comfort zone is addictive; the more you do it, the more you want to do it. You'll gain confidence in your skills, foresight, and team-building talents as you go along.

So give your latest adventure a few days to settle in, take a vacation if you need one and have the time, then start looking for your next risk. Go back to Step 1, follow this process, and see what happens. You'll discover two facts of life: you'll become better at preparing, mitigating, and thinking on your feet, and no matter how well you do all three, some risks just won't pay off. That's life. Learn, network, and keep coming back for more.

BECOME A CONNOISSEUR OF EVERYTHING

There's one final bit of risk advice that doesn't really fit into the ten steps: learn a little bit about everything. Risk divers are adventurers at heart, so even if you're risking in a particular field, you never know when some esoteric bit of knowledge that you picked up years before is going to come in handy. I recommend taking an interest in everything, from art and science to politics and law; when you have spare time, read. Subscribe to multiple magazines, from *National Geographic* to *BusinessWeek*. Become a connoisseur of everything, because at some point, some of it will come in handy.

I know this firsthand. When I was running *Capture Life,* I had to learn about page layout and graphic design. But when I went into real estate, I assumed that knowledge would gather dust and I'd never revisit it again. Boy, was I wrong; these days I use those skills to create brochures, flyers, e-mails, and more. Marketing is important to any company. Having an eye for design and knowing how to package your company in a classy way is important. I have a marketing director, but if I'm on a trip or they're not around, I can do what they can do. There's nothing anybody at my company can do that I can't. I don't have time to do everything, but I can if necessary.

There's no such thing as useless knowledge. In my time in Florida real estate, I've had to learn not just about real estate law and finance but meteorology (to deal with hurricane season), economics, and the psychology of tenants, so that I can read people more effectively. I'm learning every day from Charles and other deal makers I come into contact with. I expect to amass a broad body of knowledge. And I expect it all to come in handy at one time or another.

Don't limit yourself in your learning. Don't be like the salesperson a friend of mine told me about who, when questioned about a certain project, shot back, "I only know about things that make me money!" That's a sad, empty way to live. Risk should excite and enrich you in more ways than just your finances. Devour knowledge, because you have no way of knowing where your next risk will take you.

8.

SETTING YOURSELF
UP FOR SUCCESS

Luck is the residue of design.

JOHN MILTON, AUTHOR OF *PARADISE LOST*

Back in 1990, Mark Victor Hansen and Jack Canfield, both already successful motivational speakers and success trainers, sat next to each other on a plane. They talked about the stories they had both been collecting—stories of people's life struggles, loves, losses, tragedies, and, ultimately, personal triumphs. It turned out they had both collected hundreds of great stories that they had used for years in their speeches and presentations about self-help and personal potential. Audiences at their keynote speeches and workshops had been asking both men to compile their stories into a book, but it hadn't happened. On that flight, they decided to work together to turn those stories into an uplifting, inspirational book that Canfield named, in a moment of inspiration, *Chicken Soup for the Soul.*

Working together, Hansen and Canfield culled the hundreds of stories they both had saved down to the best sixty-eight, then asked their motivational speaker friends for more stories. In the end, they put together a manuscript of 101 stories of all kinds, from comedic tales to deeply emotional narratives of love and loss. And after three years of unrelenting work that cost them each many thousands of dollars in costs and lost work, they had their completed manuscript. Now, they had to sell it.

That proved more difficult than either man could have imagined. They knocked on the door of virtually every publisher in the business and heard the same thing from each one of them: "No thanks." Their book was a strange animal that couldn't be easily categorized, they were told. It was an anthology, which was the kiss of death for sales, they heard. It wasn't topical enough, it was too positive, and on and on. In the first month their book was circulating, thirty-three New York publishers turned them down. In all, Hansen and Canfield were shown the door by a staggering 140 publishers. In the end even their agent gave the book back to them, defeated.

Here's where the overwhelming majority of individuals would have thrown up their hands and given up, exhausted from beating their heads against the publishing industry wall and tired of getting their hopes up only to have them dashed. But to their immense credit, Hansen and Canfield did not quit. They still believed in their idea; the trick was to find someone, anyone, who shared that belief. So they regrouped. They attended the 1992 American Booksellers Association Convention, the Super Bowl of the book industry. There they found Peter Vegso, President of Health Communications, who saw the uplifting, inspirational potential in the book and agreed to publish it. The first *Chicken Soup for the Soul* book was published in June 1993.

Today, you can't blame Hansen and Canfield if they indulge in a tiny bit of private "I told you so." After being rejected by virtually every publisher in the industry, the *Chicken Soup* books have become a global publishing phenomenon, with more than seventy-five specialized titles aimed at groups from golfers to writers to mothers, and more than 100 million books sold—and counting. The *Chicken Soup* franchise has become one of the most lucrative licensed properties in the world, spawning everything from lunchboxes to audio CDs and producing hundreds of millions in revenue.

THE POWER OF PERSISTENCE

I bring this up because it's a great story of risk taking, but also because it illustrates a quality of great risk takers that I think gets overlooked: persistence. Turning risk into reward requires more than being daring, perceptive, and innovative; it means being persistent in the face of failure. Many risks will take time, more time than people realize, to come to fruition and pay off their rewards. In the world of real estate, it can be a matter of years between concept and land use plan on paper to fully built condominium community ready for sale and move-in. In between, you have permits, design review, environmental review, possible legal hurdles, engineering, and on and on. A delay can rear its ugly head at any step. It takes a clear, strong vision of what you want to achieve and the firm belief that you can achieve it in order to get past the obstacles that will appear in your path.

I've told you that I made no money during my first six months in real estate. That was depressing, but I never thought of quitting. I knew that if I kept working hard and learning, I would eventually break through. But imagine if I had thrown in the towel. I would have either gone crawling back to my former partners in the magazine and asked for my old job back, or I would have been forced to start all over from scratch selling homes for RE/MAX. I'm sure I would have been okay, but I wouldn't have had the chance to help build MyHouseRE.com into what it's become, and wouldn't have become a millionaire investor in residential properties. I wouldn't have the money to help Katrina victims put their lives back together. My life would be the poorer because I lacked the persistence to see my risk through to the end and the patience to let things fall into place for me.

That's a key lesson of risk taking: you can put all the people and pieces into position, plan until you can plan no more, and anticipate every contingency, but sometimes you just have to start the machine, let it run, and see what comes out from the other end. Persistence and patience often go hand in hand with the gung-ho, act-now attitude. Here's how it works: you see a time-sensitive opportunity, you gauge the risk and reward potential, and you decide you've got to commit fast. So you commit. You get in the game and get your pieces in place. You learn on the fly and make a plan as you go. You put yourself in a position to succeed. And then you wait. There are some things beyond your control. Often, sound risk taking means moving quickly to put yourself in the right place at the right time, and then being patient. You stay focused, believe in your goal, and refuse to quit. And you wait for the stars to align.

That's what Mark Victor Hansen and Jack Canfield did with *Chicken Soup:* created something extraordinary and then kept pushing until they found someone who saw what they saw. Their stars finally aligned, and today they are rich, successful, multi-bestselling authors.

HAVE A MENTOR OR BE ONE

I think when you take a closer look at the country's most successful individuals, you'll find that 90 percent of them have something in common: they either had a great mentor, served as a mentor to someone else, or both. Most likely both. It makes sense. How many of us come into our life's chosen pursuit knowing just what to do, the tricks of the business, the pitfalls to avoid? I think it's safe to say that almost nobody does. Even if successful people didn't have a mentor who showed them the ropes of their profession, they almost certainly had someone who taught them to think, to solve problems, or to be creative. Take any achiever in any field and I'll bet you $1,000 that at some stage that person had a mentor that he or she still remembers fondly and gratefully.

Mentoring is a concept that goes back all the way to ancient Greece. The word comes from the name of Mentor, a friend of Odysseus, the mythical Greek king who took Troy with the wooden horse as told in Homer's eighth-century B.C.E. epic poems, *The Iliad* and *The Odyssey*. In fact, one of the most renowned conquerors in history, Alexander the Great, was devoted to his mentors. As personal development author and researcher Asoka Selvarajah, Ph.D., writes, recent biographies of Alexander have pointed out that he was a devoted reader of Homer's poems, and that the Greek ideals of heroism and glory captivated and inspired him. According to accounts, Alexander saw himself as kin to the warriors who had taken Troy, and he was so obsessed with *The Iliad* that he took a special copy of the poem with him during his conquests, which covered more than two million square miles of the Mediterranean world.

Alexander particularly identified with Achilles, the near-invulnerable hero whom Alexander was supposedly descended from. Living up to the legacy of Achilles became part of Alexander's mission. As a source of inspiration and instruction, Achilles was Alexander's mentor, despite the fact that he had been dead for centuries. Even kings and emperors have people they look to for answers and guidance. Alexander also had one of the greatest philosophers and scientists of all time, Aristotle, as his living mentor and tutor, and the example of his successful warrior-king father, Philip of Macedon, to emulate. With such high-powered mentors, it's easier to understand how Alexander conquered the known world by the time he died at age thirty-three.

My mentor is really Charles Andrews, my coauthor. He taught me everything he knew about real estate and business, and I soaked it up like a sponge. He opened every single door he could for me, but left it up to me to walk through. As he likes to say, he set up the pins and I knocked them down. His enthusiasm for success was and is contagious; it rubbed off on me, got me reading every real estate book I could get my hands on, and made me hungry to learn.

IF YOU WANT TO DO GREAT THINGS, GET A GREAT MENTOR

The reason I've been talking about mentors is that this chapter of *Risk & Grow Rich* is about steps you can take to prepare yourself mentally and emotionally to locate and capitalize on worthwhile risks. One of the best things you can do toward that goal is finding a wonderful mentor, like I was lucky enough to do. Warren Buffett didn't burst from the womb a brilliant investor; he learned to become one at the feet of his mentor, Benjamin Graham.

Mentors are more than teachers. They're inspirations. One of my great inspirations in my work is Robert Kiyosaki, the author of the bestselling *Rich Dad, Poor Dad* franchise of books. He's brilliant, and his ideas have inspired me to develop my own approach to success, which led directly to this book. Not surprisingly, Charles is a devotee of Kiyosaki and has spoken with him on many occasions. Birds of a feather flock together.

It's important to have people in your business and personal life who support your dreams and your ideas and who hold you to a higher standard. Mentors are our cheerleaders and our drill sergeants, pumping us up on one hand and giving us a badly needed swift kick in the pants when we really need it. Most important, in my opinion, is that a great mentor shares his or her experience and what he or she has learned from mistakes. Mentors can teach you skills, certainly, but I believe their greatest value is in helping you develop perspective and accumulate knowledge, and in instilling you with the desire to seek knowledge for yourself. That way, instead of just soaking up facts, you're learning from their mistakes, seeking your own wisdom, and making your own fresh, new mistakes.

So my first piece of advice to you as you begin your journey as a risk diver is this: get yourself a fantastic mentor and open your ears. It could be anyone—a business colleague, a minister, a former college professor, a grandparent. A great mentor doesn't even have to be someone who's working in your field; if you want to build your fortune in real estate, you don't have to have a developer as your mentor. It doesn't hurt, but a great mentor should be someone who shares wis-

> **"Life is a fatal adventure. It can only have one end. So why not make it as far-ranging and free as possible?"**
>
> **Alexander Eliot, author and critic,**
> ***New York Post*, 1962**

dom that applies in any field, who inspires you to expect more from yourself.

Invest the time to find that person, be candid about your desire to learn
from him or her, and let the relationship grow on its own. A mentor/
mentee dynamic can't be forced; it's got to grow and flower on its own. But
if it does, open your ears and absorb. A good mentor can teach you about
assessing people, distinguishing good opportunities from bad ones, and
balancing your personal and professional lives—all skills that will make
you a more successful risk taker.

STICK YOUR TOE IN THE WATER

As I've said, risk taking becomes a habit when you do it well. However, any
leap outside your comfort zone will be unnerving or downright frightening
if you make the leap bigger than you're ready for. What I suggest to inex-
perienced risk divers is this: dip your toe in the water before you jump in up
to your neck. Acclimate yourself to the idea of risk taking by putting yourself in situations that feel foreign to you but where the risks are small.

You might also call this the "astronaut training" approach. Especially
in the early days of the U.S. space program when we were racing with the
former Soviet Union to get a man on the moon, would-be astronauts were
run through training exercises and simulations hundreds of times for years
before they went into space. The intention was to train the novelty of the
situation right out of them. NASA wanted these former daredevil test
pilots to say to themselves while in Earth orbit, "Huh! Well, this doesn't
feel so different from training!" And that's exactly what happened. Since
they weren't preoccupied with the fear and excitement that come with unfamiliar situations, they were able to focus on getting the job done and
coming home alive, which they did.

There was also within NASA the ability to think quickly and impro-
vise. On November 19, 1969, Apollo 12 was lifting off from Cape
Canaveral when lightning struck the Saturn V rocket body, knocking all
communications offline. Houston controllers were about to abort the mis-

sion when a young controller named John Aaron suggested an obscure computer command to reset the spacecraft's onboard computers, a command that only lunar module pilot Alan Bean remembered. Together they implemented the idea and communications returned, saving the mission.

Do the same thing. If you're nervous about the idea of jumping into risky situations and unsure about your ability to handle them, start small. Exit your comfort zone and insert yourself into environments where you can take small risks without major consequences. Be prepared to think on your feet. Here are some examples of what I'm talking about:

— If you've never owned stocks, buy some shares online and learn about following their progress.

— Write a business plan for your company and run it by professors in the business department of your local university.

— Pitch your company idea to an area "angel" investor group or a venture capitalist.

— Get on the interest list for a condominium community in your area. Go to the sales office, find out what it takes to prequalify, and get the details on all costs.

— Attend an auction and bid on a valuable collectible, even if you don't buy. Just get your hand in.

What do these have to do with your desires to become a real estate tycoon? Everything. Doing things like these gets you used to being outside your comfort zone, helps you think on your feet, gives you new confidence in your ability to handle the unknown. Most people don't take risks because they fear the unknown. But when you're confident that you can handle whatever situation you find yourself in, the fear becomes meaningless. In fact, it becomes a tool you can use to challenge yourself.

The key in sticking your toe in the water is that every time you do, be sure you walk away with new knowledge: a new skill, insight into a profession or lifestyle, or knowledge about yourself. Those collective lessons will be a wonderful foundation for your future success.

FIND COMPETITORS TO KEEP YOU MOTIVATED

It's tough to stay motivated, and that's especially true after you've achieved some success. I know people in my business who, once they became wealthy, stopped putting their butts out there on the line. And you know what? They became unhappy people despite their wealth. Humans need to strive and fight toward goals. It's our nature. It's your nature even if you don't realize it.

What motivates me has changed over the years. When I got through with college in 2000, I had graduated magna cum laude with a 3.9 GPA and I couldn't get a decent job to save my life. I didn't even know what kind of job I wanted. I didn't have two nickels to rub together. Up to that time, I was obsessed with controlling all factors in every situation. If you do that, you're never going to get anywhere; you're going to waste your energy trying to influence forces that can't be influenced. Even though my parents had instilled in me the belief that I could handle any risk, I still felt the need to prepare and learn everything before making a move. In my situation after college, when I was at financial rock bottom, I came to realize that wasn't going to work. I needed to embrace uncertainty and adopt more of a "go for it" attitude.

I said to myself, "It's do or die now. You can either live with Mom and Dad because you're afraid to put yourself out there and try something you know nothing about, or you can take a risk." I connected with college friends, and we talked about printing a fancy map of the Palm Beach area that would show fancy restaurants and the like. These restaurants and other business would pay to be on the map. Well, we kept expanding the map idea and making it more lavish until we finally just said, "Heck, let's just make it a magazine." I ended up starting *Capture Life* magazine, which led to my meeting Charles, which led to MyHouseRE.com. One bold, courageous choice led to a cascade of new risks and new opportunities, each of which has enhanced my life.

Back then, I took risks because I had to. Today, I take them because I *want* to. What motivates me now is goal setting—setting one goal and achieving it, then setting another one higher and achieving that. It's an adrenaline rush. You feel good about yourself. The more goals you achieve, the more willing you become to take larger and larger risks. I've now developed that confidence that I can set an idea in motion and make it happen. I've learned to control the things I can control, and to let go of the things I can't, confident in my ability to roll with the punches and handle whatever comes my way. I realized a long time ago that I had to learn to roll with the punches, so I trained myself to control what I could and not worry about what I couldn't.

But this is all about you. How can you stay motivated when you're taking your baby steps into the world of risk and reward? One of the best ways I've ever found—one I still use myself—is to find competitors who you can play off of. Each of us has someone we want to either emulate or defeat. Either way, competition is healthy. Find someone in your professional or personal life who is on the same path you're on, then use his or her achievements as benchmarks for your own progress. When your competitor makes a deal, you vow to make two. When he or she runs a half marathon, you run a full marathon, and so on. Your competitor (or competitors; you can have more than one) doesn't have to know he or she is in your sights. You can have ten competitors who don't know you exist, but who motivate you to do great things.

In my experience, it's important to choose competitors who inhabit the same world you do. A competitor should be someone with whom you're on approximately the same level of achievement. That lets you relate to what that person is doing and compete with him or her in the same business environment. Another good reason for competing with people in your orbit and not national personalities is that you'll never know the intimate details of how the big shots do their deals; half of what you learn will

PR spin. But with somebody in your local Real Estate Investors Association, you can learn the facts firsthand, so you're not competing with mor and urban legend.

FIND YOUR COMPETITORS' STRENGTHS AND TAKE THEM AWAY

There's another perfectly good justification for choosing competitors whom you know and can keep tabs on: once you see what they're doing right, you can steal their best ideas and do what they're doing better than they do.

Surprised? Don't be. If you're in the business world, this is a matter of survival. There's nothing wrong with taking what others do and doing it better. I'm not suggesting that you steal intellectual property or undermine anyone. However, approaches to problem solving or business strategies are fair game. Take what the other guys do that works, find a way to do it better, and use their best ideas to your advantage.

This is relevant because the more risks you take and the more successes you have, the more you'll find yourself playing with the big boys and girls who have the same goals you're shooting for. In my business, that might mean some other company that's in competition with MyHouseRE.com for the exclusive right to sell preconstruction condos in a particular development. In your world, competition could be someone starting a business similar to yours. In any case, you're going to have people battling you to turn the same risks into rewards. Chances are only one of you will enjoy the reward. Will it be you?

Your competition is an element of risk that can be either completely beyond your control or largely within your control. To go back to the poker reference that I used early on, let's take a look at No-Limit Texas Hold 'Em, where poker players can bet whatever they like. You've probably watched this on TV, and if you have, you've seen how the game is played by the professionals: the player with the most chips ("big stacked" in the parlance of the game) uses his money advantage to drive the action, even if he doesn't have good cards. He forces the other players to react to him, putting them at a disadvantage. More often than not he wins because his ability to be aggressive tilts the game in his favor—*even if other players consistently get better cards than he does.*

By picking competitors in your orbit, knowing them well, and keeping tabs on the things they do that work, you can improve on their ideas, avoid their blunders, and surprise them by turning their own strategies against them. You take an element of risk that was outside your control and put it largely within your control. Now you're forcing your competitors to react to you. They're spending their time fending you off instead of making aggressive moves that could hurt you. They're having meetings to worry about what you'll do next. That's one of the factors that makes Microsoft so mighty. Companies are so busy worrying about how to compete with Gates and Company that they forget to build better products than the nerds from Redmond.

What can you take away from your competitors? Plenty:

— Business strategies

— Key networking contacts

— Marketing ideas

— Ideas for gifts and special events

— People

If a competitor were trying to curry favor with a local government body, you could issue a press release announcing that your company is sponsoring a round table about undue corporate influence of elected officials. Suddenly, sucking up to the city council doesn't look so attractive. See what I mean? You take a competitor's idea and either improve upon it or counter it so it's useless. You'll end up two steps ahead of everybody else and reduce this major risk factor to a mere annoyance.

Of course, the warning here is that the other guys can do the same to you. But as long as you're a few steps ahead, it won't matter.

CREATE CONSEQUENCES THAT ARREST FAILURE

Risk can be scary. At some point in your life as a risk diver, early or late in the game, you'll want to quit. You'll have just taken a bad beating by a competitor or perhaps by blind chance. You'll be licking your wounds, maybe out a lot of money, and you'll start thinking, "Maybe that next risky venture I had in mind isn't such a good idea after all."

Slap yourself. That's the loser mentality we talked about early on. You are going to fail; it's inevitable. We all do it. What separates the big winners of the world from the bitter guys in the retirement homes who spend their sunset years grousing about what they "shoulda done" is how they handle failure. Winners don't make it personal. They don't make it a matter of their weakness or bad ideas. They find out what they can learn from it, accept it as part of their overall success batting average—in baseball, even Hall of Famers fail to get a hit seven times out of ten—and move on. Above all, they never, ever quit.

Whether it means walking away in the middle of a risky venture that has you scared to death or ditching future plans and retreating into your nice safe comfort zone to lick your wounds, quitting is worse than death for risk divers. I'm not just talking about the temporary loss of an opportunity or two. When you quit and abandon the mindset that you can jump into risk/reward situations with smarts and planning and come out on top, you take two steps back. Now it's going to be even harder to get yourself to make the leap in the future. You may never be able to make the leap again, and instead spend your life wondering what might have been. And that is a tragedy.

So don't quit. If you have to walk away from a deal because it's not right for you, find a new one and jump right back in before you lose your nerve. One of the best ways to do this is to set up consequences that will come to pass if you try to quit completely. It's aversion training for entre-preneurs. You're creating fail-safe systems that go into action if and when you try to back down from a deal that's working or lose your confidence that you can handle a life of risk taking. For me, the self-imposed conse-quence is simple but powerful: if I walk away from risk, I don't get to enjoy that incredible rush and exultation that come with the closing of a big deal. I need that adrenaline charge. I live for it. If I couldn't get it, I would wither. That's my consequence. To keep getting that buzz, I've got to keep sticking my neck out.

What could your self-imposed fail-safe be? I've seen a lot of them, and here are a few examples:

— If you show signs of quitting, your assistant brings your mentor in to give you a good tongue lashing.

— You get to take a three-week vacation in Cancun only if you close the deal. Quit the deal, no vacation.

— You give yourself a deadline. You've got to nail down a big investment by a certain date or you don't get your high-definition plasma TV.

— You announce your goal to friends and family like it's the biggest thing since the first climb of Everest. It's amazing how motivating embarrassment can be.

By doing this, you're mentally creating an atmosphere that makes it harder for you to fail. What you're really doing is setting up a series of safety nets designed to catch you during those "dark night of the soul" mo-ments when you want to give up. Although powerful, those moments don't last long, but while they are in place you might throw everything away. Consequences force you to step back and think about the situation, get some clarity and distance, and very likely shake yourself and go right back to work. If you set up your consequences right, the impetus to quit should stop dead in its tracks.

No matter how successful you get, you must always have some c̶ quences hiding somewhere in your life. When you hear about moguls li Richard Branson who are always pushing the envelope, you can bet that one of the reasons they're able to is that they've created failure-proof systems that keep them from saying, "Screw it, I'm going to buy an island and retire." They know their weaknesses. They know they're still human.

RETRAIN YOUR MIND

I've talked about retraining your mind to think of failure in an impersonal way, something that's just happenstance and not a result of personal shortcomings. That idea is at the core of the work of psychologist Martin E.P. Seligman and his principle of "learned helplessness"—people teach themselves to be helpless based on how they explain failure, either as internal and personal or as external and the result of forces beyond their control. By training themselves to explain failure differently, individuals who have spent years feeling helpless have found it within themselves to make courageous choices and change their lives. Seligman calls this "learned optimism." Even if you're one of those people who tend to say the glass is half empty, you can train yourself to see it as half full. That's an extraordinary concept: *you can change how you think.*

You can do the same thing when it comes to approaching risk. For people who are afraid to risk, the issue is always the same: fear. Their instinctive reaction to a risky situation is to look at the uncertain and the unknown as enemies that might harm them. They will back away from a possible risk before they even know the specifics behind it. Sometimes, after they've spent days gathering their courage, they come back to the risk ready to give it a shot—only to find that the opportunity has passed them by.

Others, myself included, have *consciously* trained themselves to see not the fear in risks but the potential for good. We are decisive individuals who move mountains and shape the landscape, who make others react to us. If you're going to Risk and Grow Rich, you've got to do the same thing: train your mind to see each potential risk as a positive chance to grow and gain.

u decide that a particular risk isn't for you, you'll be
to pass on facts, not fear.

in your mind to look at risk in a different way? I think
this exercise: when you approach a potential risk/
reward situation, from a real estate investment to a mountain climb, ask
yourself the following questions:

Seven Questions to Retrain Your Brain

1. What about this risk is causing me fear? (*Note:* It could be anything
    from losing money to not having physical stamina.)

2. Is my fear justified or the result of my own lack of confidence?

3. If it's lack of confidence, can I develop the knowledge or abilities I
    need to turn this risk into a reward?

4. Is there anything stopping me from developing them?

5. How will I benefit from gaining the knowledge or abilities and in
    taking the risk itself?

6. How could I lose?

7. If the benefits far outweigh the possible losses, what's stopping me?

Write down these seven questions and keep them in your purse or wallet. Memorize them. And each time you come up against a possible risk
that makes you recoil, ask yourself these questions. Does your fear make
sense? Is it just you doubting your own abilities? If it is, you're being controlled by your fear, and that's no way to live.

The more you ask yourself these questions, the more instinctive they'll
become. Eventually, your awareness of why you look at risk with fear will

become instinctive, too. You'll control your fear of risk instead of the other way around. The thought process will become natural and, eventually, unnecessary.

Look at it this way: even if you take on the risk and fall on your face, you'll have stepped outside that comfort zone. You'll have built a new comfort zone. You'll be one step closer to becoming a habitual risk diver. And take it from me, that's a great thing to be.

HAVE A SYSTEM FOR RECOVERING FROM FAILURE

There's one more bit of wisdom I'd like to share with you, something I've learned from people who've been taking risks a lot longer than I have. Just as you have a system for turning risk into reward, you should also have a system for recovering from failure. You will fail; everyone does. Those who ultimately succeed will fail multiple times, often spectacularly, but the difference between them and those who have never tasted success is that successful people do not see failure as an endpoint, but as a way station. They recover and move on, wiser for the experience.

So before we part ways, let's look at an example of a system for recovering from failure and converting it into an energy source that can propel you to new successes.

Take Pride in Your Crash

Remember, big players make loud mistakes. A monumental failure is proof that you took a monumental risk. That's something to be proud of. Instead of cowering and hanging your head in shame at your failure, hold your head up. You did something most people never do: you stuck your neck out and took a big risk. So what if it didn't come through this time? It happens. Sometimes a failure can be a blessing in disguise. The Leaning Tower of Pisa was supposed to stand straight, but if it did, would anyone venture to that corner of Italy to visit it? Of course not. It would be another run-of-the-mill *campanile* tourists pass on the way to Siena and Florence.

Celebrate your failures. More to the point, celebrate your courage and daring in going for the brass ring. Then let the failure go and move on.

Determine Your Mitigation

Remember when we talked about mitigation, setting up your risk so that even if things fall through you will reap some benefit? If you've done that, now is the time to figure out the benefit. Your risk has not paid off, but you can still walk away with something. Did you make a potentially valuable business contact? Did you discover a vendor or service provider that provides wonderful value? Did you ferret out an even better opportunity in the ashes of the one that just dug its grave? Did you discover a weakness in your own planning or get a new idea for executing your plan?

There are dozens of ways to mitigate your risk and benefit even in failure. This is not Pollyanna-style covering of your eyes in the wake of disaster, pretending everything is fine; like petroleum companies look for every way to extract oil from the land where they have a license to remove it, you should be looking for every possible way to extract benefit from your failed risk, if not from the easy-to-reach oil fields of networking or newly discovered deals, then from the oil shale and coal tar of improved planning, a clearer idea about costs, or perhaps the new knowledge that a partner is not as reliable as you thought.

Remember: sometimes failure can be a blessing. I recommend keeping an eye on the industry or project that bombed, just to see what happens. You might find some vindication in future events, like those venture capitalists who missed the investment boat in the e-commerce boom, then were the only ones left standing when Internet stocks plummeted in 2002. Finding out you were lucky to have failed won't help you find other successes, but it will make you feel a lot better!

Find the Fatal Flaw

At some point in every deal, venture, or situation, there's a root cause of failure. A source of funding doesn't come through or perhaps a decision is made to launch a store in one location versus another. In any case, every failed risk/reward scenario has what Shakespearean scholars would call a "fatal flaw." What was the fatal flaw in your plan? More important, what stopped you from seeing it until it was too late?

This is a crucial juncture in the failure recovery process, because if you don't identify your fatal flaw, you will probably suffer the same failure again. Here, I find it very useful to retrace every step in the process of taking your risk, from your initial inquiries to the final resolution. Was there something you missed? Did you or someone else on your team make a critical error in judgment? Did you fail to account for a competitor for your small business? It's very possible that the fatal flaw was no fault of your own, but correcting it should be your responsibility.

Perform a postmortem on your failed enterprise. Go back over every stage of your experience, always stopping to ask, "If I or we had done this differently, what would the outcome have been?" Look not only at your actions, but at the response to those actions. Did you launch a marketing campaign for a new business only to have it drive customers away rather than bring them in? Sometimes the response to what you did will tell you more than your actions will. With some careful detective work, you will identify the fatal flaw.

Of course, sometimes there is no fatal flaw. Once in a while, you do everything right and bad luck still wrecks your plans. But if that's the case, celebrate. That means you can go back and try again without making big changes in what you did the first time, and odds are you'll succeed.

What Did You Learn?

Every failure is a marvelous teacher. Any business mogul, inventor, artist, or leader will tell you candidly that he or she learned far more from failure than from success. So as you're doing the forensic work to figure out what went wrong, also have an eye on discovering what you learned from the experience.

Maybe you learned that your approach to risk is too reckless, or that you don't act decisively enough. Maybe you found that you were too trusting of people who ultimately let you down, or that you didn't put enough faith in the people on your team. Perhaps you discovered that you didn't know as much as you thought about accounting, real estate, or marketing and you need to educate yourself. Hidden within each failure is a lesson, a bit of insight into yourself that reveals the areas where you need to swallow your pride and learn more, work harder, or practice more regularly.

When you have found the lessons in your failure, catalog them. That way, you'll know what you need to work on before you jump back in. And if you discover that one of your failures was overconfidence or arrogance, use this as an opportunity to develop a little humility. There's no shame in not knowing everything—only in pretending you do.

EXAMPLE: The fatal flaw in Charles's NoLineGrocery.com startup was that it was an idea whose time had just not come. Added to the weakness of the e-grocery trade, the other risky aspects of the traditional grocery business— low margin, not owning your own trucks or warehouses—became killers to the business. That was Charles's introduction to the lesson that you can't outsmart a market. The market must come to you. That knowledge has served us and our clients well.

Set a New, Grander Goal

You've got the chance to go for something bigger, so why not take it? People who suddenly lose a job often take the opportunity to reinvent themselves, so why can't you? What's to stop you from setting a bigger, more audacious goal and then designing a plan to go after it? After all, you're wiser and smarter after your failure; like Thomas Edison, you haven't failed but found one more way *not* to do something. So set a grander goal to inspire yourself.

If you were planning to open one retail store, this time why not set out to open a chain? It's often easier to ask for and get large sums of money than small sums, so why not go for it? There's a very sound strategic reason for setting greater goals in the wake of failure: if you're treading new, exciting ground instead of just tramping over the soil where your last dream is buried, you're more likely to work long hours, stay up late, and stay motivated to make it happen. If your goal was to invest and retire by the time you were fifty-five, why not plan this time to retire by fifty?

Always be pushing yourself farther and asking for more. If you don't go for it, nobody's going to bring it to you.

Correct the Fatal Flaw and Make Your New Plan

This is the turning point, where you take your new knowledge about your plan's fatal flaw and your own mistakes and make things right. At this stage it's time to make a new plan for tackling your risk/reward situation, but with a keen eye on the old plan. Like an editor working on the first draft of a manuscript, you're building on the foundation of your previous work but making changes to improve it. As you plan, keep your former flaws and the lessons learned in mind. How can you prevent the fatal flaw from biting you again? How can you apply the lessons from the failure to prevent another one?

Don't treat your old plan as holy writ. If your restaurant failed because you opened it in a bad location, don't plan to reopen just down the same block. Move across town, or open a different kind of restaurant. Make fundamental, not cosmetic, changes. You may need to bring on new people and say goodbye to others. If so, do it kindly but don't worry about bruised egos; you're in this to succeed, not to make people who can't carry their weight feel better about themselves. This is the point where your success or failure in your next venture will probably be determined.

Once you have your corrected plan in place, run through it step by step, just as you did in looking for your fatal flaw. When A happens, what is B likely to be? Anticipate responses, know what you will expect from people, and know what resources you'll need in place before you need them. That's all part of sound planning for risk, and as you develop those skills, failure will become less and less likely.

EXAMPLE: I see flaws in my business processes every day. When a client calls and brings something to my attention, that's good. That means I'm able to improve it. My clients are my best editors. You don't know what your areas of needed improvement are until they smack you in the face. That's why it's important to examine and reexamine your systems. That's the way you find flaws that don't cost you or someone else thousands of dollars.

Partner with Positive Thinkers

If you're going to replace people in your plan or bring on additional people, make sure they are the type of people who do not believe in failure either. You don't want naysayers or negative individuals, but positive thinkers who, instead of seeing all the ways your plan can fall apart, see ways to make it better. There are people out there who see failure as proof of what they have always believed inside: they aren't good enough. That kind of thinking will drag you down. It will actually attract disaster to your project.

Screen the people you're working with carefully, old and new. Find those who are realistic with can-do attitudes and minds that are always looking at how things can work, not how disaster is waiting to strike. Build your team around those who have the right balance of quality skills and positive attitude.

Keep in mind, this is not to say you should bring on cheerleaders who will blindly ignore trouble or refuse to point out flaws in your plan. There is nothing wrong with criticism; it's the habit of expecting disaster that drags things down. You've heard the phrase, "Expect a miracle." Find people who expect miracles—they're the ones who make them happen.

Once More into the Breach!

Finally, when all is said and done, go for it again. Put your past failure behind you; you've already accounted for its lessons in your new plan and your new team. Act fearlessly when it's needed, with caution when it's called for, and always be observing and adjusting as things move forward.

Turning risk into reward demands flexibility, the self-honesty to know when circumstances require you to adjust your plans in directions that may not feel comfortable, but you know are right for the situation. Remember, eyes open, always.

After following all these steps and diving back in, you may fail again. Even the biggest successes have experienced multiple failures. If you do, repeat this process and go for it again. The only time you really fail is when you give up. Just ask Mr. Hansen and Mr. Canfield.

9.

A FORMULA FOR MAKING YOUR FIRST MILLION

It costs so much to be a full human being that there are very few who have the enlightenment, or the courage, to pay the price . . . One has to abandon altogether the search for security, and reach out to the risk of living with both arms.

MORRIS WEST, WRITER, *THE SHOES OF THE FISHERMAN,* 1963

I've given you principles and rules. Now it's time to give you a blueprint for making your first million. It's based on Charles's long experience in the real estate business, and I've added some of the important lessons I've learned in my career as a Realtor, property matchmaker, and personal investor. If you follow the system Charles and I have laid out, you should be well on your way to making your first million within as little as two years.

Most investors are what we call "equity rich." That means they have a lot of paper value in property that's appreciated since they bought it, but that's not real money. Just because your house is worth $1.3 million, that's not realized cash that you can do something with. But with the Equity Builder Formula™, you pull that money out of your property in equity lines and use that hard cash to do bigger and bigger deals. In this way, the money you've earned from past investments stops being abstract and starts being real money that's working for you.

IT'S NOT SPECULATION IF YOU HAVE EDUCATION

Charles wouldn't have been able to do the deals that have made him wealthy if he didn't use this basic formula. I wouldn't have bought my eight residential properties (with plans to buy more, as well as get into commercial property, where the money is even better) if I weren't tapping the equity in the property I already own.

Of course, there are plenty of people who will counsel you not to tap the equity in your real estate, saying that it's too great a risk; if the market experiences a downturn, you could end up "underwater," owing more than your property is worth. That's loser thinking. Of course you're not going to use up your equity if the real estate market in your area is stagnant or if demand is low and supply is high; that would be foolish. But if your market is strong and growing like South Florida, Las Vegas, and Phoenix, with steady migration, a stable and growing economy, job growth above the national average, and where demand outweighs real estate supply, you can do what Charles and I do and take advantage of the steady appreciation to turn equity into cash to fuel more deals.

Remember, this book is about risk, and making your first million will require risk. The Equity Builder Formula™ represents a strategy of significant risk; remember, the greater the risk, the greater the reward. However, real estate is a slow-moving investment. It's not like the stock market. You don't go to bed one night and wake up the next morning and find out your house has lost 50 percent of its value. Real estate markets are predictable; if you're paying attention to the facts and investing with your head, not your heart, you'll be able to see if your market is going to take a downward turn nine to twelve months in advance. You'll see signs like rising interest rates, properties remaining unsold longer, or stagnant local job growth. In other words, you can see what's coming early enough to make adjustments such as selling a property, backing off from a planned purchase, or increasing the rent on properties you already own.

Charles' Equity Builder Formula™ is an aggresive plan, but it's not speculation and it's not a pyramid scheme. Smart investors don't speculate; they educate. They acquire all the relevant data about the area and its properties, from job growth and future commercial development to the sale prices of comparable properties, then they buy at a recession-proof price point. Virtually any property is a sound investment *if you buy it at the right price,* such as a preconstruction condo where you get a special discount and have perhaps $20,000 in equity as soon as you take title, because when the project opens to the general public, the developer raises the price of the units. That's always going to be a smart buy. Having all the pertinent information at your fingertips, and trusting that information even when your gut tells you to be afraid of the debt you're taking on, is what will empower you to take this kind of smart risk and invest confidently, knowing you can make adjustments as things change.

FOCUS ON THE FUNDAMENTALS

If the real estate in your area is appreciating at an average of 5 percent per year, and the national average is 7 percent, that's not good. If your area is appreciating at 7 percent and the national average is the same, you are in a conservative but good market. If the forecasts for the future bring your local market above the national average (you can usually find such forecasts in the business section of the newspaper as well as by talking to real estate agents), it's a good long-term investment. If your local appreciation is *20 percent* and the national average is 7, sell whatever you have to and invest now!

But what does the future have in store? If your market is hot, will it continue at this pace, speed up, or slow down? Are you in a "bubble" market that's overheated? Are you in an underpriced market? In my experience, some markets (Las Vegas, Phoenix, and South Florida) are bubble-proof; they might slow down but they won't slide. They're simply too desirable and demand is too high. You want to position yourself in an up-and-coming market, where you get in before appreciation hits 20 percent. Las Vegas is a great example. If you started buying in Las Vegas five years ago, you've done extremely well, because the real estate market there appreciated a whopping *107 percent* from 2000 to 2005. And even though some of the hottest luxury condo properties have appreciated more than 40 percent in the last year and have slowed recently, Las Vegas's economic and job growth are the highest in the nation, with no sign of slowing down.

One of the strongest indicators of whether a market will be strong and stable over the years—and ultimately yield solid real estate investments—is the current state of the local economy of the area versus the national average and the forecast of that economy's direction. I pay more attention to economic strength and potential than I do to appreciation. The strength of the local economy means continued population growth. That means increased demand, and that means that even if prices don't continue climbing like one of the fighters my dad flew in the Navy, they're very likely to keep rising steadily.

If your local real estate market is slow moving, that doesn't mean you should just quit investing. You have to take the risk of investing in the strong markets, even if that means purchasing property that's located hundreds or even thousands of miles away. You can't wait for a market to come to you. You have to seek it out. Also, don't get hung up on appreciation. Appreciation is great, but there are many other factors that make real estate the best investment vehicle around. Mortgage interest deductions and depreciation of the property can save you thousands a year in taxes. You can rent out a unit to cover most or all of your costs and even generate some income. Real estate is not a get-rich-quick scheme, but a slow-moving, long-term wealth builder.

YOUR EQUITY SHOULD BE WORKING FOR YOU

Charles's experience and approach to real estate investing have created the Equity Builder Formula™; there's nothing else quite like it. He and I have worked together to fine-tune it into a wealth-building tool that works for most investors. It's really quite simple: you buy ten properties, using the equity from the last to buy the next. By the time you get to number ten, you have a net worth of at least a million dollars. If you're an aggressive investor, you could reach one million dollars in as little as two years. If you're more conservative, you might take four or five years. You should never invest in a way that makes you uneasy. Wealth is supposed to give you pleasure, not stress you out.

For most people, their home is their largest investment. Why? Because in recent years, they have earned more equity each year than they bring home in annual income. When that's happening, your real estate equals money working for you, instead of you working for your money. Shouldn't your real estate continue to work for you? Take out an equity line of credit or do a cash-out refinance on your home, but follow this strict rule:

KENDRA'S RULE OF RISK 16

Only use your equity to purchase assets that increase in value.

Avoid spending the money from your equity on depreciated assets—cars, furniture, anything that goes down in value. Instead, reinvest your accessible equity into tangible investments that go up in value, like real estate, collectibles, fine wine, art, and precious stones and metals. Two other important rules:

1. Lower your risk by reinvesting your equity into property within a recession-proof price point. That is determined by what is considered

affordable to the majority of home purchasers in your area. That's a rule you must follow if you're to make that first million.

2. The SunVesting Rule: follow the sun to the areas where people will be moving in the future. That's where you want to invest. Remember, you can't create a market; if your local market is depressed by poor economic prospects or your local market is overheated, invest somewhere else. Baby boomers will be driving the real estate market up over the next decade with their estimated *$2 trillion* in annual spending power. According to the 2001 census statistics, one-fourth of all baby boomers will retire to warm climates. So follow the sun. Supply and demand drive real estate prices. Invest where the demand will be highest over the longest period of time, and buy at the lowest price point available in the nicest neighborhood.

The other important factor to positioning yourself to build the largest amount of equity in the shortest amount of time is *price point*. This is directly related to the "recession-proof" strategy, and it drives home the fact that if your local market doesn't offer opportunities, you should look outside your area. For example, if you live in New York City or Southern California, where the average home sells for $500,000 and beyond, even if the economy is strong and the real estate market is appreciating, the high price point of real estate there dictates that you will have to make a large down payment and assume more risk for the property. If you had bought in a real estate market such as South Florida, where appreciation is similar but prices are lower, you could get a similar-size home for $250,000—a lower-risk price point.

Using the 10 percent down payment principle, why put down $60,000 on a $600,000 property in one market when you can put down $20,000 on a $200,000 property in another, more affordable, market and experience the same rate of equity growth? More consumers can afford to buy the $200,000 property, and your carrying costs (mortgage payments, fees, insurance) are much lower. Perhaps most important, with 20 percent appreciation that $200,000 property will be worth about $480,000 in five years, while the $600,000 property will be selling for nearly $1.5 million. A lot more people will be able to afford that $200,000 property when you're ready to sell in five years. Also, you can buy three $200,000 properties for the same down payment it would take you to buy that one $600,000 property.

EXAMPLE: Let's say you own a co-op or condo in New York City that you paid $175,000 for and it's now worth $750,000. You should access the equity in the property and reinvest a portion of it into a more affordable market where home prices are a fraction of the price that they are in New York, and hire a property management company to handle renting and property maintenance for you. That's thinking outside the box—and your immediate area. This lets you stay in the home you have now, cash out as little as 5 percent of that nearly $600,000 in equity for a down payment of 10 or 20 percent, and find another $175,000 investment in another market that will eventually become worth $750,000. Tapping such a small amount of equity would increase your carrying costs on your current home very little, and by renting your new property you would cover most or all of your new carrying costs.

With this method, your out-of-pocket risk is low and your potential for reward—equity buildup—is high. Just resist the temptation to pull out equity to go on a trip, buy a car, or send your child to college. If you're going to take on debt, use it only to acquire more assets that are increasing in value.

If you follow these rules and use the Equity Builder Formula™, you have a great chance at becoming what Charles calls "multisuccessful." That means you're building your own businesses, creating jobs and income for others, and creating multiple streams of revenue for yourself. Most successful men and women create multiple paths to wealth. But they all had to start somewhere. This is where you should start.

One more bit of advice before we hit the formula: take your business and finances personally. People will tell you that business isn't personal;

they don't know what they're talking about. Business should always be personal. If it's not, you're a clock puncher. You have to sink your passion and desire and love into your real estate business if you're going to put in the long hours it takes to make that first million. You're going to have to *live* your business to get your start. Remember, the first million is always the hardest.

THE EQUITY BUILDER FORMULA™

Step 1: Find a Good House in an Area That Is Appreciating

It can be well below the average medium home price. It can be a little rundown; it doesn't matter. Just buy a place in an area that's going up in value. Charles's first place was close to his favorite surf break on the Intracoastal Waterway. He found an FSBO (For Sale By Owner) and made a deal with a Canadian out-of-country owner to purchase his seasonal home in mid-2002. Buying on the Intracoastal Waterway practically guaranteed that this condominium would appreciate rapidly as the area around it was further developed.

Property 1

— Acquisition cost: $68,000; $8,900 down payment and closing costs

— Carrying costs (mortgage, homeowner's insurance, homeowners' association [HOA] fees, mortgage insurance): $725/month

— Financing: 97 percent loan to value (LTV) (he borrowed 97 percent of the home's value, something he could do through the Federal Housing Authority [FHA] as a first-time buyer)

This is the easiest step, but it's where you can start educating yourself about your local market, job growth, development plans and other factors that will affect appreciation. Now, at this point you're going to do three things:

1. Hold your property and let it appreciate.

2. Do relatively low-cost things that will increase its value, like landscaping or kitchen improvements.

3. Start looking around for a likely investment property.

EQUITY SCORECARD

Properties owned: 1

Carrying costs: $725

Rental income: $0

Monthly cash flow: –$725 (negative)

Equity available for investment: $0

Step 2: Open Your First Equity Line and Get Rid of Your PMI

Once your property has gained equity through appreciation (and if you're on the water or in one of those Sun Belt areas I talked about, your property will appreciate), refinance for a higher amount and cash out your equity.

Thanks to incoming development, after six months, Charles's property had already appreciated to $105,000. This incredible appreciation enabled him to do two things:

1. Take out a $50,000 equity line against the increased value.

2. Convince his lender to eliminate his PMI, or private mortgage insurance. Lenders usually require you to pay PMI when you finance more than 80 percent of a home's value, which Charles did. But it's

money thrown down the toilet, and as soon as you can get rid of it, you should. When Charles's condo appreciated to $105,000 that meant he was no longer carrying debt worth more than 80 percent of its value. That meant that by law, his lender had to drop the PMI. That saved Charles $100 per month.

But the $50,000 equity line was just a vehicle. After making three months of on-time payments, Charles asked his equity lender to extend his credit line to $100,000. Looking at the fact that his condo was continuing to appreciate at a very healthy rate, they agreed. So now, nine months after buying his condo for $68,000 (or $8,900 down and $725 a month), he had $100,000 in equity ready to turn into cash while his place continued to appreciate.

You should be able to do the same thing if your home is in an area with healthy appreciation or you have accumulated a substantial amount of equity. As this example shows, appreciation is crucial; if lenders see it, they will extend you a line of credit a very short time after you buy your home.

In summary:

— Take care of your house and watch its value increase.

— Take out a moderate equity line.

— Make payments on time.

— Get an equity line increase and you're ready to invest.

EQUITY SCORECARD

Properties owned: 1

Carrying costs: $625 (after elimination of PMI @ $100/month)

Rental income: $0

Monthly cash flow:–$625 (negative)

Equity available for investment: $100,000

Remember, your equity lines don't count as liabilities until you tap them to buy your next property. While they're just sitting there, they don't impact your net worth.

Step 3: Use Your Equity to Buy a New Home and Rent It

In mid-2003, Charles used the equity he pulled out of his condo to purchase a new property and immediately leased it, generating rental income. If you can, buy a house that's more expensive than your first: if your first was $100,000, buy for $195,000. This keeps your net worth growing. Now you own two properties, one of which is generating rental income for you.

Charles bought a single-family home in preconstruction. Through his political connections (it pays to get to know local leaders and buy them the occasional lunch), he heard that Scripps, a leading health care and biomedical research corporation, was coming to the West Palm Beach area. After learning what the presence of Scripps had done for the San Diego real estate market, and based on forecasting high demand in the area due to industry moving into the region and migration patterns to the area, he felt the house was a wise investment.

He purchased a two-story Victorian-style home in a community with cobblestone streets for $170,000, with an additional $15,000 in developer upgrades. He put 5 percent down ($9,250) and waited six months until completion. After closing, he made a few payments on the property and then leased it out to the executive chef of the prestigious Breakers Hotel in Palm Beach for $1,500 a month.

Property 2

— Acquisition cost: $185,000; $14,000 down payment and closing costs

— Carrying costs: $1,540/month

— Financing: 95 percent LTV

Today, this house is worth more than $400,000. In addition, Charles has held onto the Intracoastal Waterway condo, and at the writing of this book it had been appraised at $295,000. So for his total down payment and closing costs of just $8,900, plus the $10,000 of equity he tapped to buy house 2, he's earned $217,000 in equity to date.

In summary:

— Do your homework and find a property that shows all the signs of going up in value in the near future, such as preconstruction.

— Tap a small amount of your equity line to cover a down payment and closing costs (I recommend putting down no more than 10 percent).

— Pay for extras and improvements that will increase the home's value.

— While you're waiting to close, use your social network to find a qualified renter to occupy the house as quickly as possible after closing.

EQUITY SCORECARD

Properties owned: 2

Carrying costs: $2,125 ($625 + $1,500)

Rental income: $1,500

Monthly cash flow: –$625 (negative)

Equity available for investment: $90,000

Of course, if you live in an area like New York City or Los Angeles, it may not be smart to pursue this "buy upward" strategy there, because prices are just too high. In that case, it's time to follow the "buy in another area" approach I detailed earlier in this chapter. Starting looking online and in the real estate listing magazines for other regions, and do your economic research until you find an area that you think offers a recession-proof price point, like Las Vegas or Phoenix. That's where to buy next.

Step 4: Take Out Another Equity Line on the New House

Charles then took out a $50,000 equity line at the prime rate (the low rate banks use when they lend to each other) on his new house right after it closed. After a few months of automatic payments deducted from his bank account, he took one of his bankers out to lunch and asked for a new credit line: $100,000 at the prime rate minus .25 percent. He got it.

This is a clever way to get around some of the more onerous lender underwriting requirements. Underwriters like to see full documentation before they extend a credit line—tax returns, income statements, and so on—when you go over $100,000. But forming a profitable relationship with your banker and asking for the extension personally produces the same result and keeps your CPA from going crazy. Because Charles is incorporated, he also gets some major legal tax benefits that only business bankers typically understand. I won't go into those here, but ask your accountant (and you should have one) about the benefits of doing your real estate investing using a "corporate to corporate" model.

This essentially gave Charles $100,000 of very cheap cash in the bank and an appreciating asset that basically paid for itself every month!

Once you have purchased your second property, immediately turn around and take out that initial equity line. Once you prove you can make payments like clockwork, you'll be able to increase your equity line and have more cash on hand for your next purchase. Oh, and as Charles did, once the property has appreciated to the point where you're under 80 percent LTV (meaning you've borrowed less than 80 percent of what the property is now worth), go to your lender and insist that they eliminate your PMI. That saved Charles $150 a month on property 2.

In summary:

— Buy a property that a lender can see is due to appreciate.

— Take out a moderate post-closing equity line.

— Set up your payments to be made automatically, so they're always on time.

— Form a relationship with your lender.

— Request an increased equity line at a lower interest rate.

— Get your lender to drop PMI once you're under an 80 percent LTV.

EQUITY SCORECARD

Properties owned: 2

Carrying costs: $1,975 ($625 + $1,350)

Rental income: $1,500

Monthly Cash flow: –$515 (negative)

Equity available for investment: $190,000

As I have said before, you do not have to spend your equity money right away. It can sit there, locked and loaded, ready to use when the right deal comes along. Just having the line of credit doesn't cost you anything— only when you tap into it. The point is that you have the equity lines ready to fund your next purchase. This is where you have to learn fearlessness. You'll be tempted to think about the debt you're accumulating. Don't think that way. Think about the equity you'll be building with your next house and your next, and the rental income you'll be bringing in. Remember, even your personal residence is just a liability until you start making it work for you, generating cash to acquire more assets that increase in value.

Step 5: Locate and Buy Your Next Property

You should always be researching your next purchase. If it takes a year to find the perfect property with the right prospects for appreciation, that's fine. While you're looking, your other two properties are appreciating.

In late 2003, Charles bought a condo conversion, what lenders call a nonwarrantable condo, which means that fewer than 50 percent of the residents of the units own them. Important tip: make sure you have a lender who understands condo conversions and is willing to lend you a large percentage of the LTV ratio, such as 95 percent. This minimizes your costs going in.

Remember the story about how Charles was inspired to launch My House? This was the condo experience. He waited in line two days to buy a unit for $189,990, including $15,000 for a garage, putting down 10 percent, or $18,900. Always get the best unit you can in terms of location and view—this unit was right on the Intracoastal Waterway with a water view. You can always upgrade the interior and exterior of a unit, but you can't upgrade the view or sun exposure.

The deal took ninety days to close, which is long, but at time of closing, because the developer had increased prices, Charles already had $25,000 in equity. And this was a purchase where he was a stranger off the street! It's much better to make a purchase based on a relationship with a developer or banker. That's where the sweetheart deals come from.

Property 3

— Acquisition cost: $189,000 + $14,000 in improvements, $23,000 down payment and closing costs

— Carrying costs: $1,650/month

— Financing: 90 percent LTV

Charles had further increased the value of the unit by investing $7,000 in hardwood floors, $3,000 in granite and marble kitchen and bathroom counters, and $4,000 in a plasma TV. This might normally be "overimproving" a property (a common problem when you buy a place that you really like and forget that you're not going to live there), but in this case, all these improvements enhanced resale value. And because of the view and the location, he actually moved into the unit for a while. Today, this property is worth more than $350,000.

In summary:

— If you can, get in early on a preconstruction or conversion project.

— Find a lender who understands condo conversions.

— Get the best view and location you can.

— If you're going to do improvements, improve the kitchen, baths, and surfaces such as floors. These will add the most to your resale value and improve your return on investment.

EQUITY SCORECARD

Properties owned: 3

Carrying costs: $3,625 ($625 + $1,350 + $1,650)

Rental income: $1,500

Monthly cash flow: –$2,165 (negative)

Equity available for investment: $153,000

($190,000 – $23,000 acquisition cost and $14,000 for improvements)

Step 6: Take Out Another Equity Line and Rent Property 3

You guessed it: right after closing, Charles took out another $50,000 equity line on the new condo with a different national bank. After a few on-time monthly payments, he did two things: got his lender to eliminate his $150 PMI based on appreciation (the fact that he'd been such a good customer didn't hurt, either) and extended the equity line to $100,000. Now he was ready to pounce, whichever way the market went.

I have to say something important at this point. Looking at these negative cash flow numbers and the idea of all this equity borrowing is frightening to some people. But if you can't get past your fear, you can't take the risks that create great wealth. Robert Kiyosaki, Charles, and other brilliant investors understand a fundamental principle of investing: real estate gives you the power to put your money to work for you. You can leverage an appreciating investment to purchase more property of value and let other people (renters) pay for it for you. That's making your money work for you. Some real estate experts consider your personal residence a financial asset, but I do not. As long as you're paying for it, it's a liability. But when you tap its equity, it becomes a stepping stone to get the money to purchase your first real asset.

But you can take advantage of this wisdom only if you lose your fear of it. Do not worry about negative cash flow; if you can find the right deals at the right prices, such as condo conversions with preferential pricing, you not only get instant equity on closing, you get a lower carrying cost. When you rent, you have a good chance of having a positive cash flow. But even if you have a little more going out each month than coming in, that's okay. If you have bought in the right area, as interest rates increase, the amount you will be able to charge for rent will increase. More to the point, when you earn $35,000 in equity at closing or $100,000 in equity in eighteen months, that's real money you can tap. It's not just paper profit. Yes, you could have a year or two in your life where you have $500 more per month going out than coming in. But what if the result of that extra cost was a portfolio of five investment properties collectively gaining $400,000 in value? Is it worth spending $12,000 over two years to get $400,000 when you sell? I think so. Paper profit offsets negative cash flow. Why do you think most of the richest people in the world have amassed their wealth in real estate?

You have to be a risk taker to invest this way, because you are taking financial risks. You have to believe that in the long run, the small risk of writing a few checks to cover negative cash flow is going to yield much more in the long run. If you're going to invest in real estate, you have to be thick skinned and resourceful. You have to earn enough money that if you have a vacancy or a repair, you can carry the costs for a while. If you're worried about negative cash flow, sit down, look at one month of spending habits, and figure out how you can save money. Do you really need a car costing you $600 a month? Do you need the most expensive satellite TV package? If you want to do this, you'll learn to live with the risks, see the potential for profit and not just for disaster, and find the money you need. Remember, that first million is the tough one.

Back to Charles's deal. He moved out of the unit and back into his first condo, and used a corporate housing company to make his condo available to corporate executives who needed luxury temporary housing when they came to South Florida. This didn't provide regular monthly rent, but since corporations always pay a hefty down payment and damage deposit, it worked out about the same, about $1,800 per month.

In summary:

— Turn around at closing and take out another $50,000 equity line.

— After a few months of appreciation, extend the line $100,000 and get your lender to eliminate PMI.

— Rent your property through regular channels, but consider corporate relocation and corporate temporary housing as resources. You can find tenants and corporate opportunities at websites like these:

   – Apartments.com

   – OakwoodRentals.com

   – RentNet.com

   – CorporateHousing.com

   – Rent.com

A word about getting rid of PMI. Some lenders are understandably reluctant to give up the free money, so they'll make you jump through lots of hoops. Stick to your guns. The Homeowner's Protection Act of 1998 mandates that when you reach 22 percent equity in your home, either by paying down your principal or through appreciation, your lender must automatically terminate PMI. There are a few conditions: your mortgage must be current, you can't be considered a high-risk borrower, and you can't have other liens on the property. Learn more at www.bankrate.com.

EQUITY SCORECARD

Properties owned: 3

Carrying costs: $3,625

Rental income: $3,300 ($1,500 + $1,800)

Monthly cash flow: –$365 (negative)

Equity available for investment: $253,000

Step 7: Locate and Purchase Property 4

Getting the idea now? By locating the right properties at the right time, based on information that was available to him through relationships he built, Charles was able to build equity very quickly and leverage that equity to put over $250,000 in cash in the bank, available for when the right property came along. And it was only costing him $365 a month out of pocket for a place to live.

The next "right" property came along in mid-2004, and was an example of the "Sunvesting" concept: the fact that population movement to warmer climates increases the long-term value of the area real estate. Charles purchased a condominium on the Intracoastal Waterway with an incredible pool for $170,000, with 5 percent down.

Property 4

— Acquisition cost: $170,000; $12,000 down payment and closing costs

— Carrying costs: $1,450/month

— Financing: 95 percent LTV

The more you have, the harder it gets to resist taking some of the equity you've got locked up in these properties and spending it on yourself. Charles has to fight himself to keep from buying depreciating assets like Harley-Davidson motorcycles, art, and high-tech toys. Fight the temptation. Once you retire wealthy at forty-five you can indulge, but until you have a net worth of at least a million, they're off-limits.

By the way, property 4 is now valued at about $325,000.

In summary:

— Do your homework and find another appreciating property.

— Close for no more than 10 percent down.

— Resist the temptation to tap your equity for personal pleasure.

EQUITY SCORECARD

Properties owned: 4

Carrying costs: $5,075
($625 + $1,350 + $1,650 + $1,450)

Rental income: $3,300

Monthly cash flow: –$1,815 (negative)
(–$365 + –$1,450)

Equity available for investment: $241,000
($253,000 – $12,000 acquisition cost)

Step 8: Take Out Another Equity Line, Eliminate PMI, and Rent the Property

The pattern is starting to get predictable and boring, isn't it? Good. It's supposed to. You don't want excitement; you want methodical progress toward a million-dollar net worth.

Charles was able to rent this property quickly to a nice retired couple for $1,500 a month. They were a little tougher to please than younger renters, but they were thrilled to live on the water. Plus, older tenants tend to take better care of the property—no wild parties or beer stains on the carpet. He might have been able to get more for rent, but a big part of what we do is help people and create win-win situations. Never forget this. The more people you help, the better you will do.

As usual, Charles took out his customary $50,000 equity line on the property. After a few months of on-time payments, he contacted the lender to eliminate his $125 PMI and extended the equity line to $100,000. That's more than $340,000 of available equity (because the untouched equity from the other properties is still sitting there)—equity that can be turned into cash. That's making your money work for you.

In summary:

— Look for renters among retirees.

— Open another equity line.

— Get rid of PMI.

— Take good care of people.

EQUITY SCORECARD

Properties owned: 4

Carrying costs: $4,950 ($5,075 –$125/month PMI for property 4)

Rental income: $4,800 ($1,500 + $1,800 + $1,500)

Monthly Cash flow: –$190 (negative)

Equity available for investment: $341,000

Step 9: Keep Your Eyes Open for Great Opportunities, Then Buy

As you learn more, you'll start to try deals that you might have avoided when you were getting started. For example, in late 2004, Charles found this deal: a small condominium where the owner was willing to do an assumable mortgage: Charles would "take over" the mortgage payments for the previous owner, who was getting a divorce.

The assumable loan was $110,000 and the owner agreed to take an additional $10,000 in ten no-interest monthly payments of $1,000 each. Since $110,000 was well below market value for this house, this enabled the owners to walk away with some cash in hand (remember, always strive to create win-wins). Charles then got a quitclaim on the property in his name and filed it with his title company. Because the circumstances of the sale forced the price down, Charles earned about $30,000 in equity as soon as the title papers were filed.

A warning here: always follow up on such transactions personally. Don't leave messages. It's very easy for paperwork to go missing; don't assume and don't let someone else do it. No one else is going to make you a millionaire. The Equity Builder Formula™ is a high-velocity system for self-starters. *Never* assume. Get it done yourself. Call your title company and make sure the papers get filed.

Property 5

— Acquisition cost: Assumed mortgage, $10,000 payment to owner

— Carrying costs: $1,050/month

— Financing: Previous owner's until refinanced

This was a sweet deal, as assumables often are. People who want to have someone assume their mortgage are often what are called "motivated sellers," people who don't just want to sell but *need* to sell because of debt, death, or divorce. You should always treat them fairly, but at the same time, don't walk away from a sweet deal. Important tip: with assumable deals, always have your title company do a thorough title search to make sure there aren't any outstanding liens on the property. You've got to have clear title.

In summary:

— Keep your eyes open for unusual opportunities that represent great deals.

— Build your Power Team and include a title company you can trust to look out for your interests.

— If you do an assumable, take care of the seller; you don't want bitterness or undisclosed problems.

Today, this property is worth about $250,000.

EQUITY SCORECARD

Properties owned: 5

Carrying costs: $6,000 ($625 + $1,350 + $1,650 + $1,325 + $1,050)

Rental income: $4,800

Monthly cash flow: –$1,240 (negative)

Equity available for investment: $331,000

($341,000 – $10,000 paid to owner)

Step 10: Rent, Get That Equity Line, and Start Again!

You guessed it. Once property 5 was in Charles's name, he was able to disclose the deal to his equity lender and take out his usual $50,000 equity line, then quickly increase it to $100,000. There was no PMI to deal with because it had not been attached to the previous owner's loan. Charles then turned around and rented that small condo for $1,200 per month.

From here, you would keep making contacts, educating yourself, and keeping your eyes open for the next great deal.

In summary:

— Continue taking out equity lines and having them ready to go when you need them.

— Continue doing research.

— Continue building relationships that will bring you great deals, better pricing, and/or preferential financing.

So here Charles was at the beginning of 2005 with five properties, four with tenants and one he was living in right on the water, with more than $400,000 in equity cash in the bank, ready to be used on one opportunity or twenty. That's a sweet position to be in.

Charles has continued to buy properties, but let's take stock of where he stood after these five deals:

EQUITY SCORECARD

Properties owned: 5

Carrying costs: $6,000

Rental income: $6,000 ($1,500 + $1,800 + $1,500 + $1,200)

Monthly cash flow: –$40 (negative)

Equity available for investment: $431,000 ($441,000 – $10,000 paid to owner)

That was all achieved in two and a half years, from mid-2002 to early 2005. In that time, Charles went from buying a $68,000 condominium to owning five properties worth (at the time of this writing) between $1.5 million and $1.7 million. He has about $6,000 per month coming in just from these properties, meaning they essentially pay for themselves. And then there's his net worth just from these properties, which equals their appraised value minus his liability (mortgage and equity used):

Net worth created in two and a half years: $700,000 to $900,000

That's pure profit from just five deals, money he could make liquid tomorrow by selling his properties if he decided he wanted to jump into commercial real estate or something else. With the other, larger deals Charles has continued to close since early 2005, his net worth has easily surpassed $1 million and is probably closer to $2 million. All from a starting point of $68,000 (or an $8,900 down payment), a lot of knowledge, and some bold, fearless leveraging of equity.

YOU CAN DO THIS

If you follow the Equity Builder Formula™, you will create wealth for yourself and your family in just ten real estate deals. Never cheat or take short cuts, and you will have many opportunities. I've seen many smart, powerful people lose everything because they played fast and loose. Build wealth in slow, boring, methodical, clean, ethical business deals. The results are anything but boring.

Now, I realize that this aggressive method of investing may be too scary for some people. Fortunately, there's an alternative. If you just can't see yourself living on the edge like Charles and worrying about the "bubble" bursting, try this more conservative approach:

- Buy your initial property, the one you'll live in. Let it appreciate and take out a $100,000 equity line on it.

- Use this money to purchase two more rental properties and rent them to responsible tenants to cover most of your carrying costs.

- After two years, hold your other properties and sell one at the peak of its value.

- Let's say you walk away with $150,000 in profit. Turn around and invest that money in three down payments of $30,000 each on three new properties, keeping $60,000 to cover costs and as profit.

- In this way, you sell a property once every two or three years and use the equity to buy two more.

Over time, this approach allows you to acquire additional properties without leveraging everything you own. With each property you sell, you buy at least two more, so you're always increasing your holdings. And if the market starts to dip, you can always cash out or just hold and wait for it to pick back up in a few years. It always does.

AFTERWORD

Only when we break the mirror and climb into our vision, only when we are the wind together streaming and singing, only in the dream we become with our bones for spears, we are real at last and wake.

MARGE PIERCY
U.S. POET, NOVELIST, AND POLITICAL ACTIVIST
"THE PROVOCATION OF THE DREAM," 1976

After winning *The Apprentice 3* in May 2005, training and working long hours for Donald Trump, and overseeing the renovation and sale of his Palm Beach mansion, I'm back at MyHouseRE.com, busier than ever. Our business selling condo conversions and preconstruction projects has gone off the charts—we've been selling properties almost as fast as we can bring them to investors, and that has kept me busier than ever.

I thrive on it. I'm living my dream and building what I've always wanted to build. Our company is growing at a dizzying pace and we're already hiring new staff. The whole experience is teaching me to stretch myself, to grow beyond even *my* comfort zone.

Best of all, though, is the fact that I feel like I have a platform I can use to make a difference in people's lives, to be an inspiration. I want to be seen as a woman who steps into what has been thought of as a man's world—the world of high-risk, high-stakes business—taken big risks, and made them pay off spectacularly. I'd like women and young professionals of both genders and all backgrounds to see me and think, "I can do that. I can make my life what I want it to be." Remember, just a few years ago I was a broke college graduate with no prospects. The thought that my example could inspire others to create their own brilliant success stories keeps me going even when things get crazy and exhausting. That's what's truly important to me.

So with that goal in mind, I'd like to share with you a few final thoughts about taking risks, staying motivated, and why people who really do get out there and take big risks deserve praise and accolades, because they really are changing the world.

IT'S HARD TO STAY HUNGRY

I've found this to be true, even for me, a self-professed risk junkie. Even with all the rewards I've earned from going out on the proverbial limb again and again, sometimes it's tempting to sit back with a drink, look out over my vast empire (kidding!) and say to myself, "Why put myself through all this again? Why not just take it easy and enjoy what I have?" It is very hard to stay hungry, and the more successful you are the harder it gets.

Staying hungry matters, because it's the only way you can get yourself to spend the time on the planning, research, and preparation that turn risks into successes. It's just like star athletes. You get a young baseball, basketball, or football player who's been working hard for years to make it to the pros, then he finally gets the $50 million free agent contract. Half the time, he's going to get lazy. He won't intend to, but he's going to coast. Instead of working out in the off-season because he needs to try and keep his job, he's going to spend part of the time lying by the pool in his new mansion, hanging out with his friends and partying. Then when he comes to training camp next season, he's suddenly not in such good shape and not as great a player as he used to be.

Then there are the legends: Michael Jordan, Roger Clemens, and Jerry

Rice, to name three. What separates them from the pack? Talent? Sure. But talent, as Stephen King once said, is a dreadfully cheap commodity. No one in any field ever reached the peak on pure talent. You've got to stay hungry. You've got to keep working. That's why, every winter, opponents would cringe when they saw Jordan come to training camp with an improved jump shot, Clemens throwing harder than pitchers half his age, and Rice in incredible physical condition. These legends spent the off-season working tirelessly to get better. That's what it takes to be the best: never being satisfied. Tiger Woods is the epitome of that spirit today.

Losing your hunger is understandable. It's natural to want to bask in your success and not work quite so hard. But here's the harsh truth I have learned from personal experience: if you don't stay hungry you will *not* do the small things that it takes to remain truly successful. You won't make the extra phone call, you won't put in the extra time at 11:00 P.M. when you'd rather be in bed, and you won't care about beating your competition. You'll get "soft," which is how athletes describe a world champion team that, having won its title, no longer "wants it enough." You've got to keep wanting it.

But how do you stay hungry when you're fortunate enough to be doing well? It's something I grapple with all the time, and here are some of the tricks I've found to be successful:

— **DO WHAT YOU LOVE.** I can't overstate this. I've grown to really love real estate, and my love for it goes beyond the money. I love homes as an investment, I love finding and taking care of great tenants, I love the whole concept of investing in a place that's my favorite in the world. If you are taking risks in an area that you love passionately, you won't have to worry about losing your hunger. For example, if you've loved classic American cars since you were a kid, and your dream is to open a shop to restore those cars, then no matter how successful that shop is, you're always going to be hungry to take more risk in that area. Even if you end up with a chain of car restoration shops, a TV show, and your own magazine, you'll still have the hunger because behind it all is that passion that you'd have even if you were just restoring your own car in your garage.

— **GROW AN EGO.** It doesn't hurt to have an ego in any business. By no means should you become an arrogant jerk, but you should develop a sense of pride in what you're doing and a desire to be the best at it. I love knowing that I'm damned good at finding great residential properties, and that sense of pride keeps me from becoming lackadaisical. If I screw up a deal because I got lazy or complacent, I'm going to be furious at myself, because I've violated my own standards for excellence. Growing an ego about your own work can be a healthy thing, because you'll develop an uncompromising standard for everything you do. You become your own traffic cop.

— **KEEP RAISING THE BAR.** Goal setting is what keeps me moving forward, and nothing motivates me like a goal that's a little tougher than the one I just reached. If you've just made your first climb of a 10,000-foot mountain, do you set out to climb another 10,000 footer? Of course not. Where would the fun be in that? You make plans to scale a 12,000-foot peak, because the challenge of aspiring to something (literally) higher brings out the best in you. It's the same for any endeavor. To keep yourself hungry, keep moving the bar up. Go for a bigger deal, try to reach a new profit goal, shave ten seconds off your fastest race time, or get a new book done a week faster than the last one. It works.

— **GET ACCOUNTABILITY PARTNERS.** I love this tactic. Charles is my accountability partner and I'm his. An accountability partner is someone who is responsible for kicking you in the rear end when you make any noises about wanting to quit, wanting to take it easy, and so on. It can be a friend, it's often a colleague, but it's always somebody with a tiny sadistic streak who doesn't mind hurting your feelings. You share your latest goals with your AP, and it's his or her job to bug you, push you, and hold you accountable for doing what you said you were going to do. Some people have weekly lunches or phone calls with their APs, and if they haven't done what they were supposed to do that week and try to duck the lunch or call, the AP has permission to hunt them down like a dog and bug them until they keep their commitment. All kidding aside, it takes real caring and love for another person to be an accountability partner. You have to be a bit of boxing trainer and Marine Corps drill instructor with some Mom thrown in. A great AP will become your best business friend.

IF YOU'RE WORRIED ABOUT LOSING IT, YOU'LL NEVER HAVE IT

Risk means the chance of losing something, maybe everything. No amount of planning or preparation will change that. But in becoming a risk diver, you've got to train your mind to think positively about risk/reward situations. If your first impulse is to worry about what you might lose, you've already lost.

There's a certain state of mind that comes with being a habitual, joyful risk taker. You have to love the idea of creating something more or better than you have right now. You have to see risk *itself* as rewarding, as a force that pushes you and changes you and gives you the chance to reshape your world. To some degree, you've got to be an ascetic, willing to let go of the things you have and what you've built for the pursuit of something higher. You must be willing to lose it all to gain more.

To have this kind of attitude, you must be able to adjust your thinking about what constitutes gaining and losing. If you're a true risk diver, then the worst thing that can happen to you is to be denied the chance to push your limits. The best thing that can happen is the opportunity to challenge yourself to stretch for a goal that might be out of your reach. You won't know until you go for it. The risk itself becomes the reward because it helps you become more the kind of person you want to be. This doesn't preclude planning and preparing, of course, but closing the deal or finishing the marathon become incidental results. What ends up mattering most is that you leaped.

Does any risk taker have that pure "never worry about losing" attitude 100 percent of the time? I don't know. Maybe some of the great explorers and adventurers did, people like Amelia Earhart and Captain Cook. Sometimes I have it, sometimes I don't. But like anything else, it's something to strive for. Becoming a better risk diver is a goal in itself.

MANY CAN, FEW DO

Henry David Thoreau, in the opening to his classic book *Walden,* said that one of his reasons for building his tiny house on the shores of Walden Pond and retreating to a simple life was that he wanted to "live deep and suck the marrow out of life." That's a wonderful sentiment. Unfortunately, few people live with that kind of passion and purpose. I find that sad. Every one of us has the hidden potential to step out of our comfort zone, take even the smallest risk, and get on the road to meaningful change in our lives. But few people do it. That's what separates the risk divers from everyone else. We all have the capacity, but only risk divers take action.

I know what it took for me to become someone who acted on that potential to change things: poverty and humiliation. I was broke and embarrassed that despite a high-powered college degree I couldn't find work. I had nothing left to lose, which can be a very empowering position.

Have you ever asked yourself, "What do I have to lose if I take the risk I've been dreaming about?" What *do* you really have to lose? Time? True, but if you're not doing what you love and leading the life you desire, you're just wasting your time anyway. Money? Possibly, but money, unlike time, is something you can always get more of. And if you're barely scraping by and miserable about it, how much money could you lose in the first place? Your life or health? That depends on the risk, and those are the things you've got to be careful of. You don't want to take a risk where getting killed or terribly injured is probable, but then again you could be killed the next time you drive on the highway. The risk of injury is one of the factors that gives pursuits like skydiving and back-country skiing their attraction.

What most people really have to lose in throwing off the desperation and embracing the risk they've always dreamed of is this: *lack of accountability*. If you never take the risk, you never have to worry about taking the blame for failing. You can always make it somebody else's fault that you didn't start your business, didn't run that triathlon, didn't backpack across Africa, didn't make a million dollars. You can sit around and wait for Fate or God or whatever to take you away from all this. You never have to take the biggest risk of all: looking at yourself in the mirror after the dust clears and saying *I blew it. I screwed it up. It's my fault.*

As Thomas Edison said after an experiment that didn't yield hoped-for results, "If I find 10,000 ways something won't work, I haven't failed. I am not discouraged, because every wrong attempt discarded is often a step forward." That's the attitude of a person who intends to Risk and Grow Rich. The moment of accountability is one to savor, not fear. It's the time when you look at what you've done, right and wrong, and learn how to improve.

If you can train yourself to approach failure from that direction, there's no stopping you from taking the big risk and pursuing your dream. If you can't, then the only thing stopping you is *you*.

CHANGE IS HARD—DEAL WITH IT, MAKE SOMETHING HAPPEN

Change always hurts. Most Americans are not prepared for it. We're living in a country where constant pleasure is our chief goal and where an economy has been built on selling us things that supposedly make us happier and more beautiful. We don't handle the idea of pain very well. America wasn't always like this, but times have changed. If you're going to make that leap from your comfort zone to your dream, you're going to deal with the pain of change.

You may wake up at night worried about losing money. Friends or your spouse may become angry at you for spending more time on your venture than with them. You could lose your job. The wouldas, couldas, and shouldas of life will assault you with doubts. You'll feel at sea, like your world is free-falling and you don't know where you will land. Congratulations. Welcome to the club.

You know all those painful symptoms that appear when you decide to make a major change in your life? Treat them as signposts that show you you're on the right road. If you're not feeling uneasy, scared, or uncertain about what to do next, you're not doing enough to make the changes lasting and transforming.

That's what taking smart risks is all about. It's about changing your life, taking a step up, even if you're perfectly satisfied right now. Do you want to settle for satisfied? Wouldn't you rather be blissed out, excited, adrenaline-pumped, and stoked just to be getting up every morning? If the road to the life you want is change, then risk is the vehicle that's going to get you there.

FINAL WORDS

I'm blessed enough to finally be on my road, and to be working with some incredible people. And to think if I hadn't taken a risk that took me far outside my comfort zone, I wouldn't be where I am now. I hope that some of the lessons I've picked up on this long, strange trip will be of use to you in your journey. All I can say is:

> *Rethink failure.*
> *Find your passion.*
> *Stop worrying about losing.*
> *Plan.*
> *And go for it.*

There really is nothing you can't do.

REAL ESTATE RESOURCES

BOOKS

Rich Dad, Poor Dad, by Robert Kiyosaki, Warner Business, 2000.

The entire Rich Dad, Poor Dad franchise of books, audio and video products, also from Warner.

The E-Myth, by Michael Gerber, Ballinger, 1985 (Gerber has also created a franchise of other outstanding E-Myth books).

The Millionaire Real Estate Mindset: Mastering the Mental Skills to Build Your Fortune in Real Estate, by Russ Whitney, Currency, 2005.

Checks Don't Lie, by Mike Perl, self-published, 2006.

The Beginner's Guide to Real Estate Investing, by Gary Eldred, John Wiley & Sons, 2004.

The Millionaire Real Estate Investor, by Gary Keller, Dave Jenks, and Jay Papasan, McGraw-Hill, 2005.

Real Estate Investing for Dummies, by Eric Tyson and Robert S. Griswold, For Dummies, 2004.

Investing in Real Estate, by Andrew James McLean and Gary W. Eldred, John Wiley & Sons, 2003.

PERIODICALS

National Real Estate Investor (monthly, www.nreionline.com)
Real Estate Magazine (monthly, www.rismag.com)
Smart Money (monthly, www.smartmoney.com)
Fortune (monthly, www.fortune.com)
Kiplinger's Personal Finance (monthly, www.kiplinger.com/personal finance)
Forbes (monthly, www.forbes.com)

WEBSITES

Real Estate Investors Club, www.reiclub.com
The online directory to the nation's regional real estate investors' clubs.

National Association of Realtors, www.realtor.com
A resource for tracking home listings via the Multiple Listing Service, the tool Realtors use to promote their properties for sale.

Investment U, www.investmentu.com
Clear, contrarian, candid info about what works and what doesn't in real estate investing.

www.creonline.com
A leading information site on real estate investing.

www.johntreed.com
A myth-buster who calls out bogus investment gurus and provides a lot of solid investment information to boot.

www.preferredconsumer.com/real_estate
A soup-to-nuts portal where you can find articles, listings of real estate agents, and more.

International Real Estate Digest, www.ired.com
A portal for people interested in domestic and overseas property.

www.legalwiz.com
A useful resource for information on legal, tax, liability, and business issues for would-be investors.

www.realestateabc.com
Some basic information, more for consumers who are buying or selling a home, but some useful tidbits.

www.realestatelink.net
A gung-ho tips and resources site for the hardcore salesman in you.

ACKNOWLEDGMENTS

Kendra: My deepest, heartfelt thanks to my father, John, and my mother, Cheryl, for instilling in me the belief, from my earliest years, that I could do anything, and that to stick my neck out and take a risk was not only desirable but noble. And to my sister, Jamie, for your continuous love and support. Thanks also to Mark Burnett and Donald Trump for giving me the incredible opportunity to take the next steps toward my goals by competing in and winning *The Apprentice.*

Charles: I must thank my father Dwight Andrews, who was killed when I was eleven. When it happened, I was angry, but later I realized you made me stronger. In the military, when things got tough, I was able to persevere because something of you in me helped me endure. So I honor you, even though I never really knew you.

SunVest Communities has been our honored developer partner for many years, and MyHouseRE.com would not be where we are today without their formula for success. Many thanks to Herb Hirsch, Harvey Birdman, Nadene Birdman, and Matt Krac.

Special thanks to our staff for keeping us going during the crazy months since the end of *The Apprentice* and during the production of this book. We couldn't have done it without you.

And of course, a big thanks to the people at ReganBooks, especially our marvelous editor, Doug Grad, who took our rough-cut little stone and turned it into a polished jewel, and our publisher Judith Regan, whose vision enabled us to turn this dream into a reality.

Finally, huge thanks to our writer, editor and friend Tim Vandehey, without whose dedication, talent, and ability to wrangle us and our ideas into coherent, entertaining form on a very tight schedule this book could not have been written.